THE WAY OF THE GOLDEN SECTION

THE WAY OF THE GOLDEN SECTION
A Manual of Occult Training

John Michael Greer

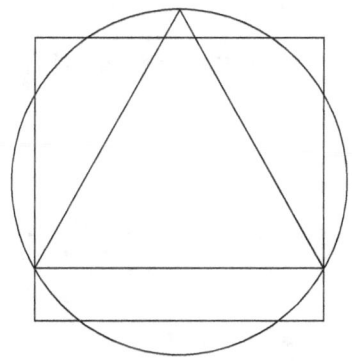

AEON

Aeon Books
PO Box 76401
London W5 9RG

Copyright © 2021 by John Michael Greer

The right of John Michael Greer to be identified as the author of this work has been asserted in accordance with §§ 77 and 78 of the Copyright Design and Patents Act 1988.

All rights reserved. No part of this publication may be reproduced, stored in a retrieval system, or transmitted, in any form or by any means, electronic, mechanical, photocopying, recording, or otherwise, without the prior written permission of the publisher.

British Library Cataloguing in Publication Data

A C.I.P. for this book is available from the British Library

ISBN-13: 978-1-91350-466-3

Typeset by Medlar Publishing Solutions Pvt Ltd, India

www.aeonbooks.co.uk

CONTENTS

INTRODUCTION ... ix
  Sources of the tradition ... xi
  How to use this book ... xiv

CHAPTER ONE: The path of occultism ... 1
  Objective and subjective minds ... 3
  Symbolism ... 4
  The one life ... 6
  The thirty-three emblems ... 15
  The outer emblem of the fellowship ... 17
  The three currents ... 18
  The way of occult training ... 20
  The meaning of initiation ... 22

CHAPTER TWO: Beginning the path ... 25
  Morning and evening exercises ... 26
  Solar plexus exercise ... 28
  Daily divination ... 29
  Affirmations ... 31
  Journaling ... 33

Your practice record	34
Your lodge and altar	35

CHAPTER THREE: The sphere of protection — 41
- Learning the ritual — 43
- Understanding the sphere of protection — 57
- Divine names and the sphere of protection — 58

CHAPTER FOUR: Meditation and scrying — 63
- The art of discursive meditation — 65
- The art of scrying — 75
- Scrying and the Sacred Geometry Oracle — 80

CHAPTER FIVE: Body practice — 83
- Aikido — 84
- Do-in — 84
- Five Tibetan Rites — 84
- Hatha yoga — 85
- Shintaido — 85
- Tai Chi Chih — 85
- Other arts — 86

CHAPTER SIX: Opening and closing a lodge — 87
- Opening ceremony — 88
- Between opening and closing — 92
- Closing ceremony — 92
- Understanding the opening and closing ceremonies — 94

CHAPTER SEVEN: The ritual of initiation — 97
- Before your initiation — 98
- Constructing the Outer Emblem — 99
- The initiation of the golden section fellowship — 103
- After your initiation — 107
- Basic practices and meditation — 108
- The initiate's morning exercise — 109
- The initiate's sphere of protection — 109
- Understanding the initiate's sphere of protection — 112
- Working in your lodge — 113

APPENDIX ONE: Exercises for the 33 Emblems 115

APPENDIX TWO: Meditations on the 33 Emblems 169

RESOURCES 183
   Occultism resources 183
   Sacred geometry resources 184
   Body practice resources 185

INDEX 187

INTRODUCTION

For more than five thousand years, since its origin in the temples of ancient Egypt, occultism—the science of the Unseen—has existed in the western world. Like everything else, it has had its golden ages and its times of obscurity, its successes and its failures; there have been times when its practitioners were welcome in the courts of kings, and other times when they were derided, persecuted, or burnt at the stake. Rationalists have condemned occultism as superstition and religious authorities have denounced it as devil worship; by and large, neither group has known much of anything about what it was they condemned, but blind hostility toward the unknown is a tolerably common bad habit among human beings.

In reality, occultism is neither superstition nor devil worship. It is a set of teachings about those things in our world that we don't experience through the five material senses. It is not opposed to science—occultists recognize that scientific research is the best toolkit our species has yet found for figuring out how matter and energy work, and only wish that scientists would notice that there is more to the world than matter and energy. It is not opposed to religion—many occultists are themselves people of faith, and pursue their occult studies and practices while still following the tenets of their religion. It is a third thing distinct from these two. You turn to science to learn about matter and energy; you turn to religion to learn about faith and morals; you turn to occultism to learn about consciousness and the unseen worlds that lie between the realm of Deity and the realm of matter.

Every so often it becomes necessary to reframe the teachings of occultism in new ways, so that those teachings can address the needs, the concerns, the hopes, and the fears of people in an ever-changing world. This book is one such reframing, drawing on the long heritage of occultism but presenting that heritage in a way that is suited to students today.

In a very real sense, this book is an experiment. Most occult schools in the past used either correspondence study or in-person teaching to pass on the traditions and practices of occultism. This book, and certain other volumes related to it, provide an open source self-study program instead. As a student of these teachings, you don't need to submit your work to a mentor or take classes. The practices given here are self-correcting and will teach you through experience. By practicing them and performing the ritual of initiation that concludes this book, you become a member of the Golden Section Fellowship.

The Golden Section Fellowship is not an organization of the usual kind. It charges no dues and hands out no certificates. The qualifications for membership are simply your willingness to take on a course of occult training. You become a member by working your way through this book, and you remain a member so long as you continue to do the practices of the Fellowship. So long as you keep up those practices, no one can expel you from the Fellowship, but if you stop doing the practices, your membership lapses at once. And if you decide to take them up again? Welcome back; the door is always open.

Occultists use the word "egregor" (pronounced EGG-ruh-gore) for a collective mind or consciousness. An egregor is created whenever a group of people share the same feelings, thoughts, ideas, or values. Nations have egregors, so do cities and communities, so do churches and clubs and businesses, and so do more temporary gatherings of people. If you've ever attended a sports game and felt some force bigger than yourself make you leap to your feet cheering when your team scores, you know something of the power that an egregor can have. The Golden Section Fellowship has its own egregor—in a very real sense, it *is* an egregor. You help to build and strengthen that egregor by doing the practices in this book, and the egregor helps to guide and strengthen you, in ways you may or may not recognize.

Sources of the tradition

Occultism includes many different traditions, schools, and lineages, no two of which have exactly the same teachings and practices to offer. It has therefore been standard for a long time for students of occultism to start by learning one tradition as thoroughly as possible, and then to study other traditions in order to fill in the inevitable gaps. That was certainly what I did! The material covered in this book thus comes from several different sources, though each element has been adapted and tested to work well with the others. Prospective members of the Golden Section Fellowship may find it helpful, or at least interesting, to know something about the traditions that contributed to the ideas and practices presented here.

The Druid revival

This part of the story begins in the early 1700s in England, where a small but significant number of people objected to the forced choice between dogmatic Christianity and dogmatic scientific materialism their society offered them. They were deeply concerned about the casual destruction of the British environment being caused by the Industrial Revolution, and they wanted a spirituality that was oriented toward nature and open to independent thought. Since no existing tradition offered that, they drew inspiration from the ancient Druids—the priests and loremasters of the ancient Celtic peoples—and took the name of Druid for themselves.

The history of the Druid Revival is complex, and may never be fully unraveled. Certainly, though, Druid organizations spread across the English-speaking world over the years that followed, reaching America by the 1790s and Australia by the 1850s. In 1912, physician and Freemason Dr. James Manchester founded the Ancient Order of Druids in America (AODA) in Boston. Manchester received a charter from an English Druid order, the Ancient and Archaeological Order of Druids and he became AODA's first Grand Archdruid. AODA was a very minor presence in the American occult scene until 1952, when Dr. Juliet Ashley became its third Grand Archdruid.

Ashley was a longtime occultist, a member of the Theosophical Society and a student of the great American occultist Manly P. Hall. By the time she was elected to lead AODA, she had already become the head of two other occult organizations, the Order of Spiritual Alchemy and the Order of Modern Essenes, and had been initiated into a third, the Holy Order of the Golden Dawn. Under her leadership, all these organizations exchanged teachings and practices in the way that occultists usually do.

The Universal Gnostic Church

Also in 1952, three American Universalist ministers—Revs. Omar Zasluchy, Owen Symanski, and Matthew Shaw—objected to the approaching merger of their denomination with the Unitarian Church, and left to form a church of their own. Like so many other religious dissidents in American history, they ended up coming into contact with occultism. In their case, it was by way of a French tradition that followed in the footsteps of the ancient Gnostics: that branch of early Christianity that valued personal religious experience (*gnosis* in Greek) over dogmatism. The denomination these three ministers founded was thus named the Universal Gnostic Church.

In 1972, Rev. Shaw moved to Boulder, Colorado and met Dr. Ashley. The two of them became close friends; Shaw was initiated into all three of the orders Ashley headed as well as the Holy Order of the Golden Dawn, and Ashley was consecrated as a bishop of the Universal Gnostic Church. It was a student of theirs, Dr. John Gilbert, who initiated me into all these organizations in 2003 and 2004, and it was from the material that I received at that time that the Golden Section Fellowship draws most of its practical teachings.

Sacred geometry

The occult and spiritual dimensions of geometry have been part of the teachings of occultism for thousands of years, but by the twentieth century sacred geometry was at a very low ebb. It was preserved in fragmentary form in the rituals of Freemasonry and studied intensively by a handful of occultists, of whom R.A. Schwaller de Lubicz was the most significant. That began to change in 1968 when British occultist John Michell published *The View Over Atlantis*, which became a runaway bestseller in the counterculture of the time. This and Michell's later books included a great deal of sacred geometry. In Michell's wake, older books on sacred geometry found their way back into print and new books on the same subject began to appear. It was one of these latter—Robert Lawlor's superb *Sacred Geometry: Philosophy and Practice*—that convinced me that sacred geometry deserved as much study as I had time to give it. It was from another source, however, that I saw how it could be combined with occultism to make a workable spiritual path for people today.

The Golden Section Order

Many years ago, in the 1970s and 1980s, one of the most innovative and interesting of the Druid groups in Britain was the Golden Section Order Society for the Preservation of Celtic Lore, Monuments and Antiquities. The Golden Section Order or GSO, as most people called it, was founded by a talented architect, occultist, and Druid named Colin Murray, who named it after the Golden Section or Golden Proportion, one of the most important relationships in sacred geometry. The GSO published a journal, *The New Celtic Review*, and a series of broadsheets which explored Celtic spirituality, occultism, and sacred geometry, illustrated by Murray's exquisite ink drawings. Unfortunately the GSO did not survive Murray's death in 1986, but some of his work was passed on to other Druid orders afterward.

That was where I first encountered the GSO and its work. One of the Druid orders in which I have been trained and initiated handed out, to initiates of a certain grade, a collection of Murray's broadsheets. Of all the many things I experienced in the course of my Druid education, the GSO broadsheets were among the most influential. It was by studying them closely, meditating on their teachings, and experimenting with them in various ways that I came to see how Druid spirituality, traditional occultism, and sacred geometry could flow together into a practical spiritual path for modern people.

The Golden Section Fellowship is not descended from the GSO in any other sense, and can claim no lineage from that source. In one sense, the Fellowship is my own original creation. In another, it is no one's creation, since the practices and teachings it passes on have been the property of many occult schools across the centuries. In a third sense, it derives its primary lineage from the group of occult traditions that Matthew Shaw and Juliet Ashley brought together in the 1970s. Even so, if not for the packet of GSO broadsheets I received in the mail from England in 1999, the Golden Section Fellowship would certainly not have taken its current form and might not exist at all. For that reason, it seemed appropriate to give the Fellowship a name that expresses my gratitude to one of the core sources of my inspiration.

How to use this book

The Way of the Golden Section is a manual for self-initiation into a tradition of occult study and practice, and into an organization, the Golden Section Fellowship, which exists at present entirely in the Unseen. If you are considering taking up the work of the Golden Section, I encourage you to start by reading the book from cover to cover. Then, if you decide to continue, begin with the first page of Chapter One and proceed from there. Each chapter builds on the ones before it, so it's important not to skip anything.

The course of training given in this book will take you a minimum of three months if you have no previous exposure to discursive meditation and the Sphere of Protection ritual, the core methods of practice taught here. If you know both of those, you may be able to accomplish the work in two months or a little less. That said, there are no prizes given out for hurrying, and no penalties for taking the time you need to do the work completely. If it takes you six months or a year to prepare for the self-initiation ritual that marks your entry into the Golden Section Fellowship, that's fine. What lies beyond that initiation—a quest for wisdom, revelation, and enlightenment using the tools of the occult initiate—is enough to keep you busy for the rest of your current incarnation.

One point should probably be stressed before we proceed. In order to follow the path of initiation presented in this book, **you will ideally need a copy of** *The Sacred Geometry Oracle* **book and card deck**. The thirty-three emblems of the Oracle deck are important symbols in the work of the Golden Section Fellowship, and divination with the Oracle is one of the basic practices. A few other requirements are covered further on. If for some reason you cannot get a copy of the deck, you will need to make one by learning each of the geometrical constructions in Appendix 1 and making a set of 33 cards with the relevant diagrams on them. This will take you a great deal of time and effort—though it is the way I made my original deck of Sacred Geometry Oracle cards, and making a deck of your own in this way is not without its rewards.

With that, the doors of the temple of wisdom stand open before you. Are you prepared to enter? If so, read on.

CHAPTER ONE

The path of occultism

From earliest times human beings have recognized that we live in two worlds at once. One of these worlds is made up of the things we can explore with our five ordinary senses. The other is made up of things that can't be encountered so easily. We can speak of these two worlds as worlds of matter and spirit, or the Seen and the Unseen. Most kinds of human knowledge deal with the world of matter, with things we can see and feel and sense, directly or with the help of instruments. Occultism is different. It is the study of the Unseen.

The word "occult" literally means "hidden." (It has nothing to do with the word "cult.") When the moon or a planet moves in front of a star, astronomers say that the star has been occulted. The things that occultists study are hidden from our senses the way an occulted star is hidden. What hides the world of the Unseen from us, however, isn't some external thing like a moon or a planet. It's internal to us. Most of us have not yet developed the inner senses that would enable us to experience the world of spirit the way we experience the world of matter.

Down through the years, many different ways of developing those inner senses have been worked out, and not all of them focus on the same set of inner senses. This book teaches one such way of development.

2   THE WAY OF THE GOLDEN SECTION

The practices and teachings in the pages ahead are meant to help you develop the power of intuition. This is exactly what the word sounds like: in-tuition, inner teaching, the inward knowledge that enables the human mind to grasp things that are normally hidden from it. The development of intuition leads to wisdom—the sense of truth that makes it possible to live in creative harmony with the world. It leads to revelation—the sudden flash of insight that reveals the unknown. Ultimately, it leads to enlightenment—the state in which wisdom and revelation are permanent conditions of the soul.

Occultism isn't a religion, but it deals with some of the same topics as religion: for example, the afterlife and the nature of the soul. Some of what occultism teaches about these subjects differs from what many religions teach—though of course religions also differ among themselves! Though some religious leaders insist that religion and occultism are incompatible, plenty of occultists are also Christians, Jews, or members of other religious traditions. Occultism doesn't teach faith and morals. If you want those, your local church, synagogue, temple, or other religious organization is the place to look.

The great difference between occultism and religion is that in occultism, there is no place for blind faith. As a student of occultism you'll be expected to learn and think about certain teachings, but you'll never be asked to believe them unquestioningly. As we'll see a little later on, furthermore, many occult teachings are meant as symbols, not as statements of fact. To understand how this works, we need to start by talking about the two minds that each of us have.

A few words about magic

These days a great many people confuse magic with occultism. That is a little like confusing marine biology with biology, or French literature with literature. Occultism is a very broad field of study, dealing with all the many ways that human beings interact with the Unseen; magic is much more specific, and mages—practitioners of magic—need to study and practice a great many things beyond the basic principles and disciplines of occultism. To put it another way, every mage is an occultist, but not every occultist is a mage.

Magic has been defined as the art and science of causing change in consciousness in accordance with will. Like the rest of occultism, it has nothing to do with superstition or devil worship. Like other forms of occultism, it uses symbols of various kinds in order to tap into the hidden powers of the mind and the universe. It requires a great deal of study, practice, and plain hard work to master.

This book will not teach you magic. The Golden Section Fellowship training is intended to give you a general grounding in occultism, not the specific training needed to get you started as an apprentice mage. On the other hand, if you are interested in becoming a mage, the training in this book will give you a solid basis in general occultism, and you can go on to other books for specifically magical training. My books *The Druid Magic Handbook* and *The Dolmen Arch* provide instruction in a system of magic that starts with the same basic practices the Golden Section Fellowship practices, and you may find them useful.

Objective and subjective minds

These two minds have various names, but in occult schools they have often been called the *objective mind* and the *subjective mind*. The objective mind is the one you're using right now, as you read these words and think about what they mean. It's called "objective" because it faces outward, toward the world of objects that you experience with your senses, and its essence is *polarity*: its world is always twofold, divided between the self and the not-self, the mind that experiences and the world that is experienced. This is the mind you use to think and reason and plan with. More likely than not, it's what you think of first when you think of yourself. It is centered in the brain.

The subjective mind, by contrast, is the mind that faces inward, toward your feelings, your intuitions, and your inner life—toward you as a subject, rather than toward the world as an object. Where the essence of the objective mind is polarity, the essence of the subjective mind is *pulsation*—the rhythm of the heartbeat, the cycle of sleeping and waking, the greater cycle that leads from birth to death and beyond. This mind is as much a part of you as the objective mind, but most people in modern societies have become estranged from it, sometimes even hostile to it. Where the objective mind is centered in the brain, the subjective mind is centered in the solar plexus—a complex structure of nerve cells behind your stomach, which functions as a second brain regulating your vital organs and your life processes.

The subjective mind is older than the objective mind: older in terms of your life, and also older in terms of life on Earth. When you were a newborn baby, long before your objective mind had its first meaningful thought, your subjective mind was already managing your heartbeat, your breathing, and all the other affairs of your body, gathering up dreams for you to dream, and beginning the process of awakening your subtle senses. Equally, far in the prehistoric past, long ages before living things first evolved brains, they had clusters of cells handling the things your subjective mind is handling in your body right now. All animals have an objective mind, however simple, as well as a subjective mind; plants, and those single-celled organisms that existed long before the great stream of life separated itself out into plants and animals, have only a subjective mind.

Having been around so much longer, the subjective mind follows age-old patterns to a much greater extent than the objective mind. You can change your objective mind fairly easily, but you can't change your subjective mind except in very slow and gradual ways. It follows its habitual patterns of thought and behavior from day to day, year to year, and life to life. It will respond to your objective mind if you learn how to send messages from one of your minds to the other, but its responses will follow its own habits and desires, not those of your objective mind.

What makes the subjective mind so important is that it doesn't just connect us to our own bodies. It connects us to other people, to other living things, and to the universe as a whole, by way of the Unseen. Have you ever watched a flock of birds wheel in the air in perfect unison, as though they were parts of a single creature? The subjective minds of the birds, flowing together in the world of the Unseen, make that possible.

Your objective mind makes you a unique individual. Your subjective mind makes you one with the universe. Both of them are essential, and finding a healthy balance between them is important in the work of occult training. Fortunately the objective mind and the subjective mind can be taught to communicate with each other. In the realm of the visible, the brain and the solar plexus are connected by certain nerves, which allow each of them to talk to the other. In the realm of the invisible, subtler connections accomplish the same thing.

Symbolism

The objective and subjective minds also differ in the languages they speak. Your objective mind speaks whatever language or languages you learned, as a child or more recently, together with a range of mental images and the like, which you also learned to associate with different ideas. Your subjective mind speaks a language of its own, which it didn't have to learn and which is the same no matter what language your objective mind uses or what experiences you had growing up. That language, the native language of the subjective mind, is the language of symbolism.

A symbol is *an image that speaks to the subjective mind*. By "image" here is meant anything you can imagine—a color, a shape, a sound, a scent, a texture, a temperature, or anything else that comes through your senses, by itself or combined with other images. Even a word can be a symbol, so long as you repeat it in a way that catches the attention of the subjective mind.

Take a moment, before you read any further, to explore the world of images a little. Imagine that you are holding a straightedge—like a ruler, but without inch or centimeter marks. Imagine that it's made of bronze: the dark copper color of that metal gleams as you hold it, and it feels cold to the touch. Imagine tapping it gently against the nearest hard surface, and hearing the sharp sound that it makes.

One helpful hint may be necessary here. In modern societies, where so many people are used to looking at pictures on screens and so few are used to using their imaginations, many people end up thinking that mental images don't matter unless they are just as visible as a picture in a movie or a video game. This isn't true at all. As you imagine yourself holding the straightedge, you may or may not be able to turn that into a vivid mental picture—and it doesn't matter if you can or not. Whether you see the straightedge in your mind's eye or simply know that it's there, it will have the same effects.

A straightedge is a symbol. So are the pen and the compass, the other two traditional tools of the sacred geometer. There are countless other things that, when made into mental images, speak to the subjective mind. In the exercises and ceremonies included in this book, you will encounter some of those symbols and learn some of the ways in which they can be used. By working with them, you'll learn to make contact with the subjective mind through them—and since the subjective mind reaches out beyond the boundaries of yourself, you'll be able to use symbols as gateways to make contact with the rest of the universe.

The one life

The first and most important symbol in the teachings of the Golden Section Fellowship is also one of the subtlest. Around the world and down through the ages, people have understood that life is not just a chemical oddity that happens to show up in certain lumps of matter called living things. Life is a force, and it is present in all things, whether or not we usually think of them as living. Like the other forces in the universe, it flows from place to place, gathering here, dispersing there, surrounding us, penetrating us, binding the universe together.[1] It is the power behind healing arts such as acupuncture and martial arts such as aikido, and it also lies behind many of the legends of magic and miracle in the legends of the world.

The life force has countless names. The Taoist healers, and martial arts masters of China call it *qi* (pronounced *chee*); their equivalents across the sea in Japan call it *ki*; the yogis and mystics of India call it *prana*; the Hebrew prophets called it *ruach* (pronounced *roo-akh*). In Europe in the Middle Ages it was called *spiritus*, which is the source of the English word "spirit." Wherever else you go, as far back in the past as you want to reach, you can find a word for the life force—with one very narrow set of exceptions. As far as anyone knows, in all of history, the only human languages that don't have a common word for the life force are the ones that are spoken in the countries of the modern industrial West.

In the Golden Section Fellowship we refer to the life force as the One Life. Pause for a few minutes, before you read any further, and imagine the One Life. Feel your own body, alive and sensitive, and imagine that the life you feel in your body doesn't stop at your skin. Life flows out from you into the universe, and back into you from the universe. Imagine the currents of the One Life flowing through you, connecting you to everything else there is. Then let go of the image and begin reading again.

What you've just done is a simple form of working with a symbol. You filled your objective mind with an image that speaks to the subjective mind, held that image for a while, and then let go of it. Was it all in your imagination? Of course, but it won't stay that way. By concentrating on the symbol of the One Life, your objective mind asked your subjective mind to begin to pay attention to the life force. If you repeat this practice—or, more to the point, a slightly more advanced version of this

---

[1] If this reminds you of "the Force" from those famous science fiction movies, it should. George Lucas borrowed the concept of "the Force" from Japanese martial arts, where it is called *ki*.

practice, which will be covered in Chapter Two—your subjective mind will start doing this as a matter of course, and your objective mind will begin to notice the life force, too. With regular practice, you'll develop the ability to sense the flows of life force clearly. That ability will help you with a wide range of spiritual and practical activities, some of which will be explored in the pages to follow.

The three principles

The One Life expresses itself in three basic ways, and in occult teachings these ways are called the Three Principles. These Principles have varying names in different schools of occult philosophy. The names used in the Golden Section Fellowship come from the Druid Revival tradition mentioned in the Introduction, but it is helpful to learn some of the other hames, too, so that you can make sense of writings from other traditions of occultism and spirituality.

Calas, the first principle

The first of the Three Principles is called Calas (pronounced CAH-lass), and it is the principle of substance. In the writings of the alchemists it is called salt, though this term should be taken symbolically rather than literally—it isn't the same kind of salt you sprinkle on your food! In the teachings of the Hindu sages in it called *tamas*, and among the Taoists of China it is *di*, the principle of Earth. It is the expression of the One Life that makes things solid and resistant, and it is the source of matter. It can be imagined as earth with plants growing in it; its color is green, and its symbol is the square.

Diagram 1-1.

Gwyar, the second principle

The second of the Three Principles is called Gwyar (pronounced GOO-yar), and it is the principle of transformation. In the writings of the alchemists it is called sulphur. In the teachings of the Hindu sages it is called *rajas*, and among the Taoists of China it is *ren*, the principle of Humanity. It is the expression of the One Life that makes things flow, change, come into being and pass away again, and it is the source of life in the usual sense of that word, the kind of life we experience in ourselves and other living things. It can be imagined as flowing water; its color is blue, and its symbol is the triangle.

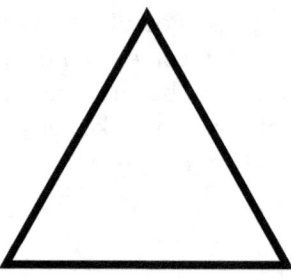

Diagram 1-2.

Nwyfre, the third principle

The third of the Three Principles is called Nwyfre (pronounced NOO-iv-ruh), and it is the principle of consciousness. In the writings of the alchemists it is called mercury. In the teachings of the Hindu sages it is called *sattva*, and among the Taoists of China it is *tian*, the principle of Heaven. It is the expression of the One Life that brings about perception, intelligence, wisdom, and enlightenment, and it is the source of mind. It can be imagined as clear air full of light; its color is gold, and its symbol is the circle.

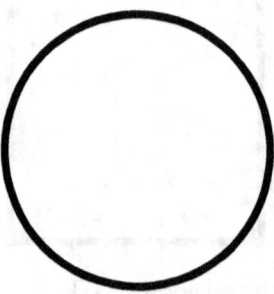

Diagram 1-3.

The seven gates

The Three Principles, as important as they are, are very abstract and general. For practical purposes, it is often more useful to work with a larger number of more specific symbols. One of the most common sets of symbols in occult practice is made up of seven gates, rays, realms, or cantrefs—this last is a Welsh word that means "district" or "region"—which are created by taking the Three Principles alone or in combination, as shown in the diagram and table below.

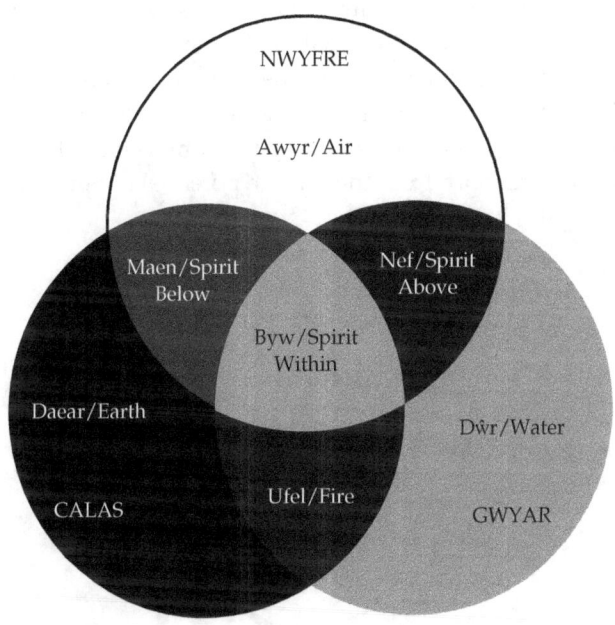

Diagram 1-4.

Table 1-1: The Principles and the Elements

Calas	produces Earth
Gwyar	produces Water
Nwyfre	produces Air
Calas + Gwyar	produces Fire
Calas + Nwyfre	produces Spirit Below
Gwyar + Nwyfre	produces Spirit Above
Calas + Gwyar + Nwyfre	produces Spirit Within

Each of the Seven Gates has its own symbolism. Not all the symbols may make sense to you at first glance, and some may be completely unfamiliar. Don't worry about this. Their meaning will become clearer to you as you proceed in the work of occult training.

The First Gate: Awyr

This Gate represents the Principle of Nwyfre by itself. It is symbolically placed in the eastern quarter of the world, the place where the sun rises, and this sense of light shines throughout the Gate and its imagery. It is the Gate of inspiration and illumination, of mind and thought. Morning, springtime, and every other image of newborn light and life correspond to this Gate, and so does inspiration and illumination of every kind. Its symbol is a circle with a line extending up from its top. This represents light and air being born from the infinite potential of Spirit. Its name is pronounced AH-wur.

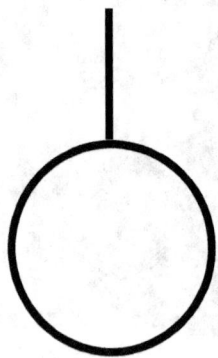

Diagram 1-5.

Among elements, it is Air.	Among planets, the Sun.
Among seasons, Spring.	Among directions, East.
Among times of day, morning.	Among colors, yellow.
Among beasts, the hawk.	Among trees, the birch.
Among days, Sunday.	Among planes, the mental plane.

The Second Gate: Dŵr

This Gate represents the Principle of Gwyar by itself, and is symbolically placed in the western quarter of the world. It is the Gate of growth, learning, and enlargement, as well as that of emotions and of all things watery. Wisdom in the old Druid lore is symbolized by a salmon who dwells in a sacred pool over which hazelbranches hang, and through this symbol water has close symbolic connections to trees and other growing things. Its symbol is the triangle pointing down, representing water's downward movement. Its name is pronounced DOO-r.

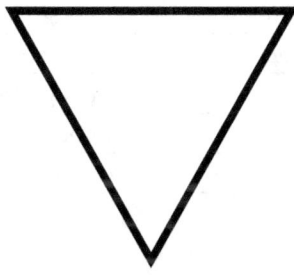

Diagram 1-6.

Among elements, it is Water.	Among planets, Mercury.
Among seasons, Autumn.	Among directions, West.
Among times of day, evening.	Among colors, blue.
Among beasts, the salmon.	Among trees, the hazel.
Among days, Wednesday.	Among planes, the etheric plane.

The Third Gate: Ufel

This Gate represents the Principles of Gwyar and Calas combined, and is symbolically placed in the southern quarter of the world. It represents every force and factor that energizes and transforms, making the many into one. It teaches us that no barrier separates us from the creative energies that weave the world into being, just as no barrier separates our energies from their broader context in the universe around us. In the unawakened self, it is passion; in the awakened self, it is intentionality. Its symbol is the triangle pointing up, representing the upward movement of flame. Its name is pronounced IH-vel.

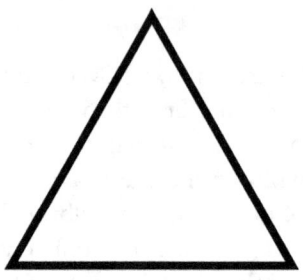

Diagram 1-7.

Among elements, it is Fire.	Among planets, Mars.
Among seasons, summer.	Among directions, South.
Among times of day, noon.	Among colors, red.
Among beasts, the stag.	Among trees, the holly.
Among days, Tuesday.	Among planes, the astral plane.

The Fourth Gate: Daear

This Gate represents the Principle of Calas by itself, and is symbolically placed in the northern quarter of the world. It is the realm of manifestation, the firm material basis that allows the other elemental powers to take form in the universe of our experience. In the individual, it is the body, and every form of embodiment and structured manifestation. In nature, it takes the shape of soil and the other materials of Earth's surface; the realm of Earth's far depths belongs to the Fifth Gate instead. The symbol of this Gate is the creative circle of spirit with a line descending downward into manifestation. Its name is pronounced DYE-ar.

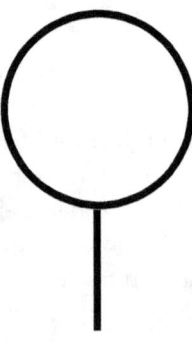

Diagram 1-8.

Among elements, Earth.	Among planets, Venus.
Among seasons, Winter.	Among directions, North.
Among times of day, midnight.	Among colors, green.
Among beasts, the bear.	Among trees, the apple.
Among days, Friday.	Among planes, the material plane

The Fifth Gate: Maen

This Gate represents the Principles of Nwyfre and Calas in combination, and is symbolically placed in the depths. It is the power of Spirit Below, and its closest representation in the world of ordinary human experience is the deep places of the earth. The world that human beings inhabit consists of four overlapping spheres, one each of fire, air, water, and earth—the upper atmosphere corresponding to fire; the lower atmosphere to air; the seas, rivers, lakes and groundwater to water; and the solid crust of the planet, to earth. Below that lies a realm as alien to human life as the furthest reaches of outer space, a realm of unimaginable heat, pressure, and energy that drives the continents across the face of the planet and sets the land trembling with earthquakes. The symbol of this Gate is the circle of Spirit with the cross of balanced manifestation below it. Its name is pronounced MINE.

Diagram 1-9.

Among elements, Spirit Below.	Among planets, Saturn.
Among seasons, time past.	Among directions, Below.
Among times of day, night.	Among colors, orange.
Among beasts, the white dragon.	Among trees, the yew.
Among days, Saturday.	Among planes, the spiritual plane.

The Sixth Gate: Nef

This Gate represents the Principles of Nwyfre and Gwyar in combination, and it is assigned to the heights. It is the power of Spirit Above, and its nearest representation in human terms is the universe beyond the limits of the earth. Just as the world we inhabit, with its four elemental spheres, stops a few miles below our feet where the earth's crust gives way to the mantle, it stops a few miles above our heads at the borders of space. Beyond these are the vast reaches where stars and planets circle through the void. The symbol of this Gate is the circle of Spirit with the cross of balanced manifestation above it. Its name is pronounced NEV.

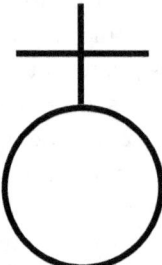

Diagram 1-10.

Among elements, it is Spirit Above	Among planets, Jupiter.
Among seasons, time to come.	Among directions, Above.
Among times of day, day.	Among colors, purple.
Among beasts, the red dragon.	Among trees, the oak.
Among days, Thursday.	Among planes, the causal plane.

The Seventh Gate: Byw

The Seventh and last Gate represents the combination of all three of the Principles, and it is assigned to the center, the point of balance in the middle of all six of the other Gates. It symbolizes the presence of life and spirit within everything in the world, including you and me. Where some religions see human beings as something set apart from the rest of the world and equally far from the divine, occult teachings recognize that human beings are part of one great reality, along with everything else there is. The symbol of the Seventh Gate is the circle of Spirit with the cross of balanced manifestation in its center. Its name is pronounced BE-oo.

Diagram 1-11.

Among elements, Spirit Within.	Among planets, the Moon.
Among seasons, eternity.	Among directions, Center.
Among times of day, this moment.	Among colors, white.
Among beasts, the human being.	Among trees, the mistletoe.
Among days, Monday.	Among planes, the divine plane.

The thirty-three emblems

Alongside the One Life, the Three Principles, and the Seven Gates, the work of the Golden Section Fellowship relies on another set of symbols: the thirty-three cards of the Sacred Geometry Oracle, which provide thirty-three emblems divided up into three Circles of eleven emblems each. It may already have occurred to you that One Life plus Three Principles plus Seven Gates equals eleven; if you noticed this, you've grasped one of the inner keys to the Sacred Geometry Oracle.

That key has to be used with knowledge, however, because each Circle has a different arrangement of the symbols. In the First Circle the symbols are in the order of generation, showing how the One Life unfolds its possibilities in making the world we experience. In the Second Circle the symbols are jumbled together, as we find them in the world around us. In the Third Circle the symbols are in the order of regeneration, returning and arising from the world of experience to the One Life. All three of these arrangements have lessons to teach, and you will explore them in meditation later on.

The first circle

1: The Unmarked Card (Potentiality/Hiddenness): the One Life.
2: The Point (Beginning/Commitment): Nwyfre, the Third Principle.
3: The Line (Extension/Separation): Gwyar, the Second Principle.
4: The Circle (Continuity/Repetition): Calas, the First Principle.
5: The Ellipse (Flow/Adjustment): Awyr, the First Gate.
6: The Vesica Piscis (Union/Encounter): Dŵr, the Second Gate.
7: The Equilateral Triangle (Form/Limitation): Ufel, the Third Gate.
8: The Hexagram (Balance/Conflict): Daear, the Fourth Gate.
9: The Cross (Interaction/Dissension): Maen, the Fifth Gate.
10: The Right Triangle (Proportion/Restriction): Nef, the Sixth Gate.
11: Quadrature of the Circle (Integration/Isolation): Byw, the Seventh Gate.

The second circle

12: The Square (Manifestation/Inertia): Maen, the Fifth Gate.
13: The Octagram (Cooperation/Compromise): Nwyfre, the Third Principle.
14: The Dodecagram (Completeness/Complexity): Nef, the Sixth Gate.
15: The Tetrahedron (Energy/Disruption): Ufel, the Third Gate.
16: The Octahedron (Mediation/Dispersal): Awyr, the First Gate.
17: The Icosahedron (Receptiveness/Passivity): Dŵr, the Second Gate.
18: The Cube (Stability/Rigidity): Daear, the Fourth Gate.
19: Square and Diagonal (Generation/Consequences): the One Life.
20: Gnomonic Expansion (Expansion/Excess): Gwyar, the Second Principle.
21: The Spiral (Unfolding/Diminishing): Byw, the Seventh Gate.
22: Alternation (Approach/Imperfection): Calas, the First Principle.

The third circle

23: The Double Square (Regeneration/Risk): Awyr, the First Gate.
24: Progression of Roots (Evolution/Unexpectedness): Dŵr, the Second Gate.

25: Discontinuous Proportion (Relation/Dependence): Ufel, the Third Gate.
26: Continuous Proportion (Correspondence/Necessity): Daear, the Fourth Gate.
27: The Golden Proportion (Harmony/Justice): Maen, the Fifth Gate.
28: The Pentagram (Power/Responsibility): Nef, the Sixth Gate.
29: The Dodecahedron (Transcendence/Transmutation): Byw, the Seventh Gate.
30: Unity of Primary Roots (Reconciliation/Paradox): Calas, the First Principle.
31: The Sphere (Infinity/Unknowability): Gwyar, the Second Principle.
32: Squaring the Circle (Attainment/Impossibility): Nwyfre, the Third Principle.
33: The Human Canon (Unity/Diversity): the One Life.

You don't have to memorize these symbolic patterns now. Later on, you may choose to do so, because they add another level of richness to divination with the Sacred Geometry Oracle, and they also help explain some of the details of the work ahead.

The outer emblem of the fellowship

Another element of symbolism you should be familiar with before we proceed is the Outer Emblem of the Fellowship. This is the circle-triangle-square emblem found on the title page and cover of this book, on Card 32 of the Sacred Geometry Oracle, and on the back of every card in the Oracle deck. It contains more symbolic meaning than a casual glance reveals. First of all, of course, it represents the Three Principles—the circle of Nwyfre, the triangle of Gwyar, and the square of Calas, in a balanced relationship and sharing a common center.

Take a closer look, however, and you may notice that there are eleven points in the diagram where lines cross. Once again, these represent the One Life, the Three Principles, and the Seven Gates. As shown in Diagram 1-12, these are assigned beginning with the One Life at the uppermost point—the only point of intersection that is outside the square of Calas—and proceeding clockwise from there.

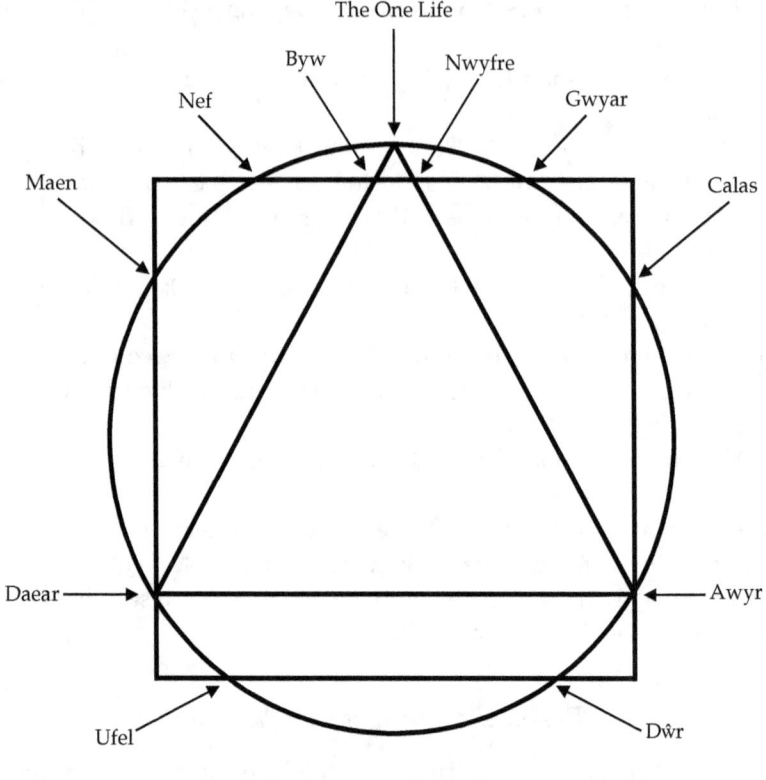

Diagram 1-12.

A great deal can be learned by studying this diagram and meditating on the relationships of points, lines, and shapes, but that can be left for your own explorations later on. For now, simply familiarize yourself with the symbol. You will need to construct it using geometrical methods as part of the preparation for your initiation into the Golden Section Fellowship.

The three currents

Finally, on a more practical level, it's important for you to know about certain specific ways that initiates of the Golden Section Fellowship relate to the One Life. While the One Life is in everything, its presence is easier to contact in some things than in others. Two things in particular, the sun and the earth, are reliable and overflowing sources of the life force. It's for this reason that some occult teachings speak of a solar current descending from above and a telluric current rising up from below.[2] Some systems of occult training use the solar current exclusively, while others work exclusively with the telluric current. Some, finally, work with both currents. The Golden Section Fellowship is one of this last category.

The solar current comes quite literally from the sun; it flows through space to the earth's upper atmosphere and descends from there to the surface. It is governed by time; it increases and decreases in any given place according to the position of the sun in the sky. It is strongest at dawn and noon, but it is present even at midnight; it flows wherever light from the sky can reach, and even reaches a short distance down into the soil. The other planets of the solar system reflect the solar current to earth just as they reflect the sun's light, and their interactions with the solar current are the sources of the influences that are tracked by astrology. The solar current's traditional symbols in myth and legend are birds such as the eagle, the hawk, and the heron. Occult writings call it *aud* or *od*. It is symbolically masculine, and one of its names is the current of knowledge.

The telluric current comes from the center of the earth. It rises up through the crust to the surface, and it is shaped by place the way the solar current is shaped by time. Underground water affects it very strongly, and springs where water comes to the surface are powerful sources of this current; so are large healthy trees, whose roots draw up water from deep underground. The serpent and the dragon are the most common symbols of the telluric current in myth and legend. Its names in occult lore include the secret fire, the dragon current, and *aub* or *ob*. It is symbolically feminine, and one of its names is the current of power.

Occultists, as an essential part of their training, learn to draw one or both of these currents into themselves for various purposes. In the Golden Section Fellowship, we learn to work with both of them. Partly this is done in order to bring about balance and healing, but it also has a deeper, secret possibility—for there is a third, secret current, the current of fusion, which is also called the lunar current.

The lunar current does not exist naturally in the individual human being or in the world. It has to be made by the fusion of the solar and telluric currents. It is shaped neither by space nor by time but by states

---

[2] The word "telluric" comes from Tellus, an old name for the earth.

of consciousness. Its symbols in myth and legend include the egg, the jewel, the sacred cup, and the child, and it is called *aur* or *or* in occult writings; it is also the secret behind the legend of the Holy Grail. When it awakens in an individual, it opens up the inner senses and grants wisdom, revelation, and enlightenment. When it awakens in the land— a far more difficult task, but one that was once done quite regularly in the days when occultism was well known by ancient priesthoods—it brings fertility and plenty. In the work of the Fellowship, we begin with the individual, but the broader possibilities of the lunar current should be kept in mind as you proceed through this book. Not all those possibilities will be spelled out. You will have to search for some!

The way of occult training

Now that you've learned a little about the symbolism used by the Golden Section Fellowship, it's time to talk about how these symbols are put to work in the quest for wisdom, revelation, and enlightenment. Most people in the modern Western world, as mentioned above, are aware of their objective minds but not of their subjective minds. They're literally going through life with half as much mind as they were born with. Obviously, that's a problem, and it explains a lot of the trouble the world is in these days: we need both our minds, not just one, to make sense of the many challenges we face as human beings.

Some popular philosophies and spiritual systems like to respond to this situation by going to the opposite extreme: insisting that the objective mind is bad and that the goal of spiritual training is to live entirely in the subjective mind. You can recognize these philosophies and systems by their rhetoric—"The mind is the slayer of the real, slay thou the slayer!" is a typical saying in such schools—but also by the practices they teach. These focus on silencing the objective mind: for example, by repeating a single word or phrase over and over again, or by passively watching thoughts arise, rather than thinking about them. People who succeed in these practices end up no better off than they started. They, too, go through live with half as much mind as they were born with; the only difference is that they've discarded a different half. They may have profound spiritual experiences, but a great many of them have a hard time functioning in the ordinary world.

A useful maxim points out that the opposite of one bad idea is usually another bad idea. Somewhere in the middle lies the point of balance, where new possibilities open up. This is the way that occultism approaches the relationship between the objective and subjective minds. In the course of occult training, we learn to use both our minds, not just one. Through study and the kind of meditation that's traditional in occult schools—discursive meditation, which directs and focuses the thinking mind rather than silencing it—occult students become better able to use their objective minds. Meanwhile, through ritual, divination, and other ways of working with symbols, occult students learn to work with their subjective minds as well, and begin the process of teaching the two minds to communicate with one another, and to work together for the betterment of the whole self.

The process of learning to use both minds isn't something that can be done in a hurry. It takes time, patience, and regular practice. While nerves connect your brain and your solar plexus, and subtler connections link the objective and subjective minds in the world of the Unseen, you will have to learn how to use those connections in ways that are unfamiliar to you. That learning process will require you to challenge some of your beliefs about yourself, and to learn a range of skills that don't always seem as though they have anything to do with the goals of wisdom, revelation, and enlightenment. Only after you've been following the path of occultism for some time will it be clear to you why every step you took was necessary.

The way of occult training can be divided into three broad phases. First comes the phase of preparation, which involves learning the various activities you will be using in your training, establishing a regular practice, and picking up enough skill that you no longer need to concentrate on getting all the details right and can begin to use the practices for their intended purposes. In this part of the work, the objective mind takes the lead, and the subjective mind continues in its ways, unaffected by your work. This phase therefore corresponds to Calas among the Three Principles.

The second phase is the phase of interiorization, which involves turning your attention inward and coming to terms with what you find there. As your practices become habitual, they begin to reach the subjective mind, and it typically responds at first by trying to shake off the unfamiliar influence. This is the phase in which your meditations are interrupted by annoying thoughts, sudden itches, or a powerful urge to fall asleep. This is when you can't remember the words of a ritual or the meaning of a card you had by heart fifteen minutes earlier, or you realize suddenly at the end of the day that you've completely forgotten to do your practices! Dealing with this phase requires patience and a sense of humor, as your objective and subjective minds struggle their way toward an unfamiliar balance. Change is the hallmark of this phase, and therefore it corresponds to Gwyar among the Three Principles.

The third phase is the phase of illumination. In this phase your subjective mind comes to terms with the work of occult training, and begins to cooperate with it. Inner change stops being something you have to struggle to achieve, and becomes something that unfolds naturally so long as you continue with your practices. Difficulties fall away with so little effort that you may not even notice their departure until long after they're gone. This phase represents a significant shift in consciousness, and so corresponds to Nwyfre among the Three Principles.

And then? You're back to the phase of preparation, but with a much clearer idea of what the practices can do, and insights into how you can make them work better for you. You can expect to cycle through the three phases many times over the course of your occult training, and each cycle will take you further and unfold more of your potential for wisdom, revelation, and enlightenment. Each is a portal, and as you pass through it you will find new portals before you, waiting to lead you even further.

The meaning of initiation

Regular study and practice are the keys to the occult way, and nothing can substitute for them. Occult schools learned long ago, however, that it's possible to make the first stages of the way of occult training a little less challenging and more productive by starting the work in a particular way. This is the way of initiation. By combining certain basic practices with a ritual that uses symbols to speak to the subjective mind, initiation can give the beginning occult student the equivalent of a running start on the journey ahead.

Broadly speaking, there are two ways to provide that running start. The first, called *lodge* or *temple initiation*, requires an organized group of trained initiates who can select suitable candidates, guide them through the necessary preliminaries, and perform the initiation ceremony for them. This is a very effective approach when an aspiring occultist can find such a group, and the group is competent and ethical. Unfortunately there aren't many such groups publicly accessible in the

Western world just now. Even more unfortunately, not all the groups that advertise themselves are either competent or ethical. This is why so many students of occultism these days choose the other option—the way of *self-initiation*.

In self-initiation, as the word suggests, the beginning student of occultism works through all the preliminary stages and performs the ritual by himself or herself. This is a slower process, since among the things the student must learn are the skills needed to perform the ritual of initiation! It also requires careful selection of practices and training exercises, because not all of these can be done safely without the guidance of a more experienced occultist. For example, the more intensive kinds of work with the centers of the life force along the spine are risky without close supervision by someone who knows what to do if something goes wrong.

Fortunately, there are practices that are safe to perform unsupervised, and centers and channels of the life force that anyone can use without risk. In the pages ahead you will learn a carefully chosen sequence of exercises and practices to prepare yourself for your ritual of self-initiation. If you follow the instructions precisely, you will learn everything you need to know to begin the way of occult study and practice, and you will perform a ritual of initiation that will give you a head start on the work before you. It will take you between two and three months to accomplish the process of self-initiation, but the skills and practices you learn in that period can be used successfully to follow the occult path for the rest of your life.

As an initiate, though, you will have taken only the first few steps toward the goals of wisdom, revelation, and enlightenment. The word "initiation," after all, literally means "beginning," and an initiate is therefore a beginner—someone who has begun the grand adventure of the occult way. The Golden Section Fellowship is a fellowship of those who have begun. Each practice you perform, each book of occult wisdom you study, each hour you devote to the work of occultism takes you further inward, on a path that leads to light and knowledge beyond your furthest imagination.

With that goal in mind, let's begin the work.

CHAPTER TWO

Beginning the path

The path of occult training requires a certain amount of work. That's true of anything worth doing, of course. If you want to become a musician, for example, you need to put in plenty of hours practicing on your instrument, and if you want to become a martial artist, you should plan on showing up at the dojo and practicing punches and kicks three nights a week. Occultism is similar. To pass through the process of self-initiation, begin your work as an occultist, and start on the path toward wisdom, revelation, and enlightenment, you'll need to set aside a certain amount of time every day for study and practice.

The practical work of the Golden Section Fellowship falls neatly into two groups. The first consists of a set of relatively simple practices that take just a little time to do each day, and can be fitted in here and there around the rest of your daily schedule. The second consists of the two main practices you'll be learning—a ritual called the Sphere of Protection, and a type of meditation called discursive meditation. For these, you'll need to set aside a period of twenty minutes or so each day, preferably early in the morning before breakfast, in which you can do the ritual and then meditate.

Both the Sphere of Protection and discursive meditation need to be learned in a step by step fashion, and they will be covered in Chapters Three and Four of this book respectively. The simpler practices are among other things easier to learn, and this chapter will walk you through the process of learning how to make them part of your life.

You'll need a few things to do the practices in this chapter. Some of them—the items you'll need to set up your lodge—are described further on. For the time being, you'll need a deck of the Sacred Geometry Oracle cards, and the book that goes with them; other books on spiritual or occult subjects, which you can choose yourself; and two notebooks or blank books. One of these is for journaling. The other is for your practice record: the chronicle of your adventures on the occult path, which you'll begin to write as soon as you begin your first practice. Both of these are described in detail later in this chapter.

Morning and evening exercises

The first exercises to take up as you start getting ready for your initiation are among the easiest. One is done every morning, as soon as possible after you get out of bed, and the other is done every evening, as late as possible before you lie down and go to sleep. Simple as they are, they should not be neglected, because they help orient your consciousness in constructive directions and lay foundations on which other practices can build.

Morning exercise

The morning exercise is very straightforward. Stand in front of a window—an open window, if the weather permits—and stretch upwards, raising your arms and stretching out your fingers. Try to stretch every muscle in your body. Rise up on your toes if you can! Then relax, lower your arms, and breathe in a slow deep breath. Hold the breath for a little while, and then let it out, making the breath long and slow. Leave your lungs empty for a little while, and then breathe in another slow deep breath. Do this seven times in all, and then go on to the rest of your morning activities.

What counts as "slow" and "deep"? That depends entirely on personal factors such as the size of your lungs and the pace of your metabolism. Don't make it so slow that you end up gasping for air. Keep your breath easy and smooth as you draw in and let out the seven breaths. With a little practice, you'll find a rhythm that works well for you.

Once you've done the morning exercise for a week or so, it's time to add another element: an affirmation. Affirmations are one of the basic tools of modern occultism, and will be discussed in more detail later in this chapter. You can make a start with this affirmation right away, though. On each of the seven breaths, as you breathe in, repeat silently: "I breathe in life from the One Life of the Universe." As you breathe out, repeat silently: "It strengthens and inspires me in all that I do." While you repeat the first set of words, imagine the One Life streaming into you with the breath, filling you with light and power and vitality. While you repeat the second set of words, imagine that light and power and vitality shining out from you like rays from the sun, filling everything in your life with a special blessing.

One other common habit of occultists is also worth adding to your morning routine. Before you eat or drink anything else, drink a mug of plain hot water, as hot as you can comfortably drink it. Most of us drink too little water and too many other things that are not as healthful to the body. Many occultists find that one cup of hot water, taken first thing every morning, helps their digestion and improves their physical and emotional health. Try it!

Evening exercise

Every evening, just before going to sleep, take a few minutes to read a page or two from a book of occult or spiritual teaching. Too many people go to bed with their worries and troubles at the forefront of their minds. This can make it hard to get to sleep, but it also has unwanted effects on the inner, occult side of things. During sleep, when the objective mind is dormant, the subjective mind ponders the experiences of the day and opens to the Unseen, and these two processes—which take place at the same time—give rise to our dreams. Whatever was in your objective mind just before sleep provides a basis, like the grain of sand in an oyster shell, around which your subjective mind builds dream-images like pearls. The old custom of sleeping on a decision before making it is one way of drawing on this same habit of the subjective mind.

Over time, as it gets used to weaving spiritual or occult themes into its dreaming, your subjective mind will make these part of its habitual patterns, and it will begin to access higher spiritual realities in sleep.

Have you ever had the experience of going to sleep brooding over a problem, and waking up the next morning with the solution in your thoughts? Your subjective mind did that—and it can do that with the great problems of human existence.

Once you begin the practice of discursive meditation, as described in Chapter Four, that can be combined with the evening exercise in a useful way. Discursive meditation works with symbols or short texts, training the mind to think as well as to focus. Each evening before you go to bed, select the theme of the next morning's meditation—the symbol or text you will be meditating on—and read it carefully if it is a text, or study it closely and then think about it if it is a symbol. Have that in your mind as you go to bed. While you sleep, your subjective mind will think about the theme, and provide you with additional insights and understandings when you meditate on the theme the next day.

Solar plexus exercise

Once you have made a habit of the morning and evening exercises, you can add a simple exercise for waking and energizing your solar plexus—the seat of the subjective mind. This is good for releasing unnecessary tensions as well. It takes just a few minutes and can be done at any time of day or night, so long as your stomach isn't too full of food.

First, sit in a comfortable chair or sofa, or lie face up on a bed. Take a few moments to relax as much as you can. Then draw in a deep breath and push out your stomach as you do so. This allows you to draw the air down into the very bottom of your lungs.

Second, without breathing out, suck your belly in and push your chest out, moving the air from the lower to the upper part of your lungs. Push your belly out again and let your chest fall, sending the air back down. Do this twice more, so that you've sent the air from the lower lungs to the upper lungs and back again, without breathing out. Then, finally, let the breath out. Let yourself go completely limp, and breathe slowly and comfortably for a little while.

Third, repeat the same sequence—breathing in, sending the air up and back three times, and breathing out—twice more, so you have done the whole sequence three times, relaxing and breathing easily between each sequence.

Fourth, when you have finished, draw in and let out three slow gentle breaths. As you do so, turn your attention to your solar plexus:

the center of your subjective mind, the mass of nerve tissue just below your ribcage and just behind your stomach. Imagine it shining warm and golden, like a little sun inside you. Feel the golden light spreading all through your body. When you have finished the three breaths, let go of the image and go about the rest of your day.

During the time you spend working on this book, the solar plexus exercise should be done once each day, at whatever time is convenient to you.

Daily divination

The next practice to add to your daily schedule is a daily reading using the Sacred Geometry Oracle cards. This is in addition to any reading you may do for other purposes. It should be done, if possible, early in the day, and it uses a particular pattern or layout of cards, rather than the freeform method taught in The Sacred Geometry Oracle.

Each morning, shuffle the deck thoroughly, and deal out three cards. If you are a religious person, feel free to say a prayer before shuffling and dealing, asking Deity to assist you in understanding the cards correctly.

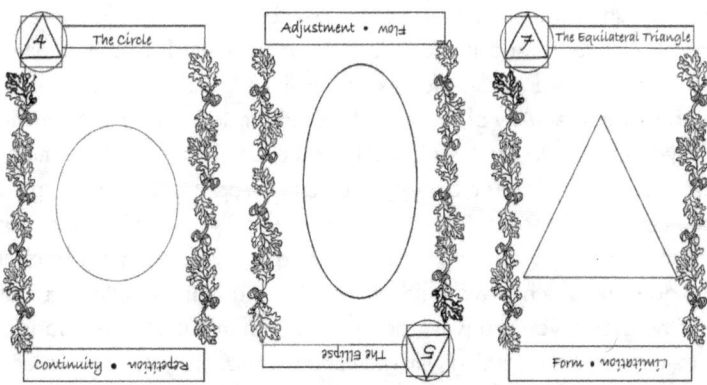

Diagram 2-1.

The first card represents you. The second card represents the situation you face that day, and the third represents the outcome. Study the cards, look up their meanings in the book if you need to, and try to foresee how that pattern of cards might work out in the day ahead. Write down the cards, their meanings, and your guesses in your practice record, as explained later in this chapter, and then go about your day.

That evening, or the next morning before you cast your next daily reading, look over what you wrote down, think back over the day just past, and see if you can figure out what the reading was trying to tell you. You may recognize at a glance what it meant, you may be left completely puzzled, or you may figure out some parts but not others. Whichever of these happens, you are beginning the process of learning to use your intuition. Over time, you will find it easier and easier to figure out what the cards are saying, and eventually you will be able to use your intuition directly, without having to shuffle and deal cards. For the time being, though, the cards are to your intuition what weights are to the bodybuilder: tools you can use to strengthen yourself, so you will be better able to deal with the challenges and possibilities of life.

> ### Other divination oracles
>
> *The Sacred Geometry Oracle* provides some of the core symbolism of the Golden Section Fellowship, but there are many other methods of divination you may also choose to work with as you pursue your study of occultism. The tarot is perhaps the most famous and widely used of these, but there are other divinatory card packs such as the Lenormand pack and the ordinary poker deck of 52 cards, which have been used as divination tools for centuries. There are also methods of divination that don't require card packs—for example, the Norse runes and the Irish Ogham alphabet. Any of these can be used for daily divination practice.
>
> If you choose to work with a different oracle, use the same method described above for *The Sacred Geometry Oracle*: cast a reading with three cards (or runes or Ogham letters or what have you) and interpret it, write down the reading and interpretation, and then go back the next day and see how you did. As you keep up this practice day after day, the oracle you use will teach you how to interpret its messages.
>
> Before you start working with a different divination system, however, it's a good idea to get a basic level of skill with *The Sacred Geometry Oracle*. You should plan on working with it for at least a year before you try something else—and once you start working with something else, you should plan on working with it for at least a year, so that you get past any initial frustrations you may have with it, and get some sense of what it can do. Patience and perseverance are essential skills for the occultist in training.

Affirmations

Another basic item of occult training you may choose to add at this point, or later on, is the use of affirmations. Affirmations are among the simplest of occult practices, but "simple" does not mean ineffective! They make use of the connections between the objective mind and the subjective mind to reshape your habitual pattens of thinking, feeling, and noticing, so you can let go of habits that don't benefit you and take up new habits that do.

You can get some sense of the power of affirmations by thinking of the habit of negative self-talk so many people have. When you make a mistake, do you say or think negative things about yourself—"I can't do anything right," "I'm so stupid," or something like that? The more often you do that, the more mistakes you'll make, because when you repeat words like those over and over gain, your subjective mind hears you and it believes what you say. Many people make their lives thoroughly miserable by doing this.

Affirmations take the same effect and turn it the other way around. When you repeat an affirmation, your subjective mind hears you and believes that, too. The affirmation doesn't have to be true to begin with—for example, if you have a lot of trouble with anxiety, you can use an affirmation such as "I am calm and focused and in control of my life." That may not be true when you start working with it, but it will become true as you continue. Repeated over and over again, it becomes a symbol—a symbol made of words, thoughts, and emotions—that communicates with your subjective mind and helps orient it toward some change you have chosen to make in your life.

Certain rules for effective affirmations have been worked out by occultists over the years. Follow them and you can get the same good results that so many others have.

Rule 1: Effective affirmations focus on a single subject. Most of us have many different things we'd like to change about ourselves, but it's important to take them one at a time. Choose one thing you want to change, focus your efforts on that, and go on to other things once you've succeeded.

Rule 2: Effective affirmations are single sentences. The longer and more involved an affirmation is, the more likely it is that your subjective mind will be confused by it. Make it simple, straightforward, and to the point, and you'll get better results.

Rule 3: Effective affirmations are in the present tense. If you put things in the future tense—say, "I will be calm" rather than "I am calm"—your subjective mind will take that literally, and the calmness you seek will always be in the future, not here and now where you need it. For the same reason, don't say "I want to be calm" or anything along the same lines. That won't make you calm, it will just make you want to be calm even more than you already do.

Rule 4: Effective affirmations avoid words like "no." Remember, we're talking about affirmations, not negations! Affirmations work best when they focus on what you want to achieve, rather than what you want to let go of. Avoid words like "no," "never," "not," and anything beginning with "un-" and you'll get better results.

Rule 5: Effective affirmations focus on changing your inner life. One of the two most common mistakes beginners make with affirmations is to try to use them to change the world, instead of using them to change themselves. You have far more power over your inner life than you do over the world. By changing habits of thought, feeling, and attention in your inner life, however, you can change the way you relate to the world around you, and that can have astonishing effects on your outer life. If you're having trouble meeting your financial needs, for example, instead of trying to use an affirmation to get the world to give you money, you might use one like this: "Everywhere I look I see opportunities for making money." It's the ability to spot opportunities that makes one person a successful entrepreneur, while others walk on by and miss their chance. Cultivate that ability through an affirmation and follow up on the opportunities you notice, and your financial troubles will soon be over.

Rule 6: Effective affirmations start small and build from there. The other of the two most common mistakes that beginners make with affirmations is to start off trying to use them on big, tough, tangled issues, heavily freighted with emotion and as often as not burdened with memories of past defeats. That way lies certain failure. Instead, start with small issues that don't have a lot of emotional energy attached to them. By succeeding with those, you build the habit of success, and that will allow you to move on to more challenging issues.

Rule 7: Effective affirmations are repeated many times every day. If you only repeat an affirmation a few times, your subjective mind won't hear it. If you repeat it a hundred times a day, every day, your subjective mind will sit up and take notice. It's worth cultivating the habit of using an affirmation to fill otherwise wasted minutes—for example, when you're standing in line at the grocery, waiting for a bus, or what have you, repeat your affirmation. If you have the habit of negative self-talk mentioned earlier, it's also worth learning to catch yourself, and start repeating your affirmation instead.

How many affirmations should you work with at a time? That varies from person to person. To begin with, though, it's best to work with one or two only. The affirmation that goes with your morning practice—"I breathe in life from the One Life of the Universe; it strengthens and inspires me in all that I do"—should be kept up all through the period you spend working with this book. You can simply use that affirmation, or you can work with that one and one other, chosen to help you make some change in your inner life you feel you need. Later on, when you're familiar with the way affirmations work and have picked up some skill with them, you can decide if you want to try to work with more than two.

Journaling

Affirmations are a simple but effective way to talk to your subjective mind. A conversation won't get far, though, if there's a way to talk but no way to listen! There are various ways to listen to your subjective mind, but one of the simplest and most useful is the practice of journaling.

For this, you'll need one of the two journals mentioned earlier, a pen or pencil, and a quiet place where you won't be interrupted for a time. Take a moment to relax, and then write down a *prompt*—that is, a question or comment about which you'd like the advice of your subjective mind. It can be something you want to understand about yourself, like "Why do I always get nervous around cars?" It can be something you want to understand about your world, like "Why is it that wherever I work, there always turns out to be a bully in the office?" It can be something much less specific than these, like "Something feels really off today and I don't know what." Whatever your prompt is, write it down.

Then, on the line below it, write the first thing that comes into your head. Write it down without leaving anything out, no matter how silly, or pointless, or embarrassing, or ugly it may be. Remember that nobody but you will ever see a word of it. Write it down, think about it, and then go down another line and write your response to it. Then, once again, write down the first thing that comes into your head. Repeat this, and let it turn into a dialogue, like this:

You write: **Something feels really off today and I don't know what.**

The first words that come to mind are these: *The old woman at the bus stop.*

What about the old woman?

The ruler in her hand.

This puzzles you, because you dimly remember the old woman and she wasn't carrying a ruler. You write: **I don't remember the ruler.**

The answer: *Yes you do. Mrs. Jespersen. Third grade.*

All at once you remember your third grade teacher, a bitter old woman who took out a lifetime of frustration on the children in her classes, hitting them hard across the knuckles with a ruler. You hadn't thought of her in decades, but the old woman at the bus stop reminded you of her, and—yes, that was when your mood crashed, for no reason you could name.

Some journaling sessions are as quick as that; some are much longer and more complex. Sometimes you won't get any answer at all, and sometimes you may get so much that you fill up pages with things that come pouring into your mind. Not everything you'll get is accurate, for your subjective mind is no more infallible than your objective mind. It can misunderstand things and misremember them, especially when strong emotions are involved. Listen to what it has to say, though, and you can learn a great deal.

How often should you practice journaling? That depends on personal factors, but at least once a week is a good minimum, and many people find that a few minutes of journaling every day helps keep the channels of communication open between the objective and subjective minds, and can clear away many of the emotional tangles left behind by unfinished business in the past.

The morning and evening practices, daily divination, affirmations, and journaling—those are the introductory practices of the Golden Section Fellowship. As soon as you begin work on them, you should start your practice record.

Your practice record

This is simply a diary, journal, or daybook in which you record the practices that you do each day, and anything you noticed about them or learned from them. Keeping a practice record is an important part of your preparation for initiation. Writing down an account of your practices helps you focus your attention on what you are doing and what you are learning from it. During periods when it doesn't seem as though you're making any headway at all, it can be very helpful to read back over your practice record and see how far you've actually come.

Most people find that it's best to write down each practice as soon as possible after doing it, so that you don't get behind and don't lose any of the details. You don't have to write lengthy descriptions of your practices in your practice record. Something like the following is entirely adequate:

July 21, 2020

>*Morning practice: I felt really sleepy while doing this, but got some sense of the presence of the One Life all around me.*
>
>*Daily Divination: 8 reversed, Limitation; 11 upright, Integration; 2 upright, Beginning. I think this means that I need to focus on wrapping up existing projects today so that I can begin something new in the near future.*
>
>*Affirmation: repeated my current affirmation, "I am calm and focused and in control of my life," while waiting for light rail on the way to and from work today. It seems to be helping.*
>
>*Journaling: didn't make time for this today. I need to be more regular about this.*
>
>*Evening practice: read a few pages of* Mystery Teachings from the Living Earth *before going to sleep. It was from the chapter on the Law of Flow, and when I went to sleep I dreamed about floating down a river in a raft!*

Once your basic practices are under way and your practice record is started, it's time to assemble the handful of things you'll need to go on to the rest of the work: the Sphere of Protection ritual, the practice of discursive meditation, and the more complex ceremonies you need to know to perform your own ritual of initiation later on.

Your lodge and altar

Much of the work you will be doing as you proceed through the rest of this book takes place in a lodge of the Fellowship. This doesn't mean that you have to run out and buy or build a lodge building! Your lodge is simply a place where you carry out the practices of the Fellowship. It can be as simple as a spare corner of a bedroom or study, and you can use it for other purposes when you're not doing rituals and practices there. There are four requirements for a lodge:

Privacy—when you are doing practices or lodge work, you need to be free from interruption. A room with a door you can close is quite adequate.

Space—the work of the Fellowship does not take up much room, but you will need enough space to turn around in a circle with your arms stretched out, without hitting anything.

A Chair—the meditations and some of the other practices of the Fellowship are done seated in an ordinary chair. A folding metal chair or a chair borrowed from around the kitchen table is perfectly suitable for this purpose; your chair should not be overstuffed or padded. It can be put away or taken somewhere else when you are not using it.

An Altar—this sounds much more complex than it is. The altar of the Golden Section Fellowship is a flat surface between waist height and shoulder height, at least a foot deep and two feet wide, on which certain things can be placed. You can use the top of a waist-high bookshelf, a bureau, or a dresser for your altar. The one additional requirement is that it needs to be located so that you can sit in your chair facing it, with nothing else in the way and a few feet of space between you and the altar, as shown in Diagram 2-2.

Diagram 2-2.

BEGINNING THE PATH   37

The altar needs to have a few things placed on it. First is an altar cloth. This can be any convenient piece of fabric of whatever color you prefer.

Next are three small bowls or containers—some members of the Fellowship like to use miniature brass cauldrons of the sort that can be found in import shops, but any small open container a few inches across will be fine. One of these is half full of salt, one is half full of water, and the third is half full of sand, on which incense can be burnt. (If for any reason you can't burn incense, fill this third bowl half full of dried flowers, dried herbs, or an herbal pot pourri that you like; the symbolism will work just as well this way.)

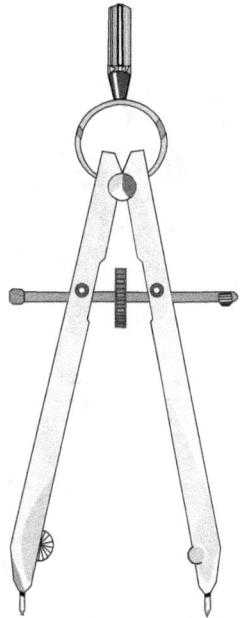

Diagram 2-3.

Diagram 2-4.

38   THE WAY OF THE GOLDEN SECTION

Finally, you will need the two traditional tools of sacred geometry, the compass and the straightedge. The compass is the kind you draw circles with, not the kind you use to find North! For a straightedge, it's usually most convenient to use a short ruler. You will need a compass and a straightedge to practice sacred geometry, and you can put these on your altar when you're not using them; alternatively, you can have a special set purely for altar use. It's sometimes possible to find ornate antique compasses in antique stores and thrift shops, and one of these can be very well suited to your altar. These are used in the Opening and Closing Ceremonies, which you will learn later on.

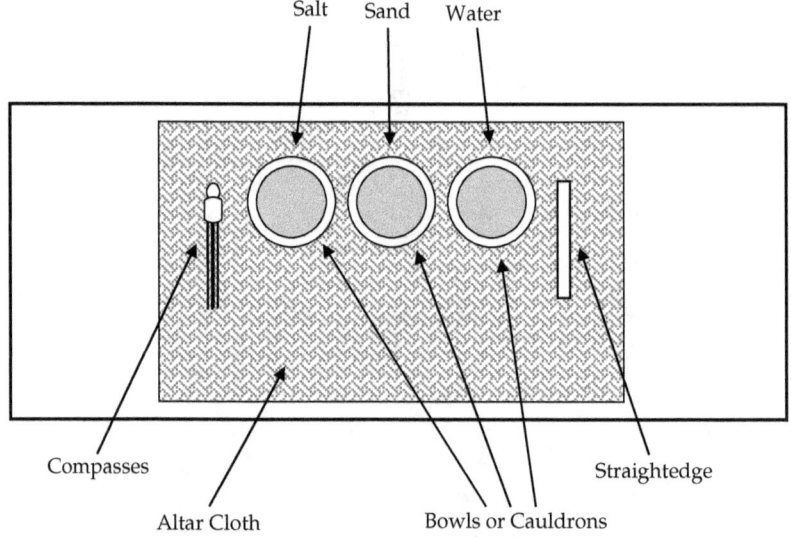

Diagram 2-5.

Your altar should be arranged as shown in Diagram 2-5. The altar cloth goes atop the altar. On it place the three bowls or cauldrons—the one half full of salt on your left as you face the altar, the one half full of water on your right, and the one half full of sand for incense in the middle. The compass goes on the left just outside the salt, the straightedge on the right just outside the water. (When your lodge is open, you'll move the compass and straightedge to the middle of the altar and put them in a certain position, but we'll cover that later on.)

You can also put other things on your altar if you like. For example, your Sacred Geometry Oracle deck can go on one side of it, and anything else that feels appropriate to you can be put to one side or another also. Leave the area in front of the three bowls or cauldrons clear, though. You'll need it for some of the work ahead.

CHAPTER THREE

The sphere of protection

The first of the more complex practices you should learn at this stage in the work of self-initiation is a basic ritual called the Sphere of Protection. Most occult schools teach some ritual of this kind, for workings of the sort you're about to do have a twofold purpose. On the one hand, they balance and strengthen you by bringing in beneficial influences from the Unseen and clearing away harmful ones; on the other hand, they teach you skills that will be essential to your further work in occultism.

The Sphere of Protection has its own complex history. Rituals of this kind have been part of occult training since ancient times, but innovation is just as important in occultism as tradition. Dr. Juliet Ashley, an American occultist of the twentieth century, used several older rituals as inspiration for the earliest form of the Sphere of Protection, which she crafted sometime around 1950. Later, in the 1970s, her student John Gilbert reworked the Sphere of Protection while pursuing a degree in theology in the Universal Gnostic Church, and developed several different versions of it over the years that followed.

John was one of my teachers and initiators, and it was from him that I learned the ritual in 2003. I had practiced other rituals of the same general type for many years, but found the Sphere of Protection to be more balanced and flexible than any other. Just as John adapted Juliet Ashley's ritual, I have adapted it further—and in the pages that follow, you will be shown how to adapt it to your own spiritual needs.

One of the distinctive features of the Sphere of Protection is that you don't start doing it all at once. It consists of three sections—an Opening, a Closing, and a set of elemental Callings in the middle. When you first start practicing the ritual, you practice the opening and closing sections by themselves, and do this for a week. You then add the elemental Callings one at a time, giving a week to each one. The process of learning the Sphere of Protection thus functions as a basic initiation into the work of the seven elements.

Seven elements? Yes. In the Golden Section system we recognize and use seven elements. The seven elements are Air, Water, Fire, Earth, Spirit Below, Spirit Above, and Spirit Within, and they correspond to the Seven Gates discussed in Chapter One. Most people who have encountered occultism know at least a little about the first four of these. Many have also heard of the element of Spirit. Spirit, however, has three forms, and in the ritual you will be working with each of these, as well as the four material elements. The Seven Gates and seven elements unfold from the Three Principles discussed earlier—Calas, Gwyar, and Nwyfre. Each of the seven elements is formed from one, two, or three of the principles, as shown in Diagram 1-4 and Table 1-1 on page 9.

Spiritual powers

One of the things that sets the Sphere of Protection apart from many other rituals of the same kind is that it leaves students free to invoke whatever spiritual powers they personally revere. That's one of the central values of the Universal Gnostic Church, the tradition in which the Sphere of Protection originated, and it also has a central place in the Golden Section Fellowship, which inherits part of that tradition. As discussed earlier, occultism is not the same thing as religion. What you do in the religious sphere of your life—the sphere that deals with the spiritual planes above human consciousness—is distinct from what you do in your occult training, and the two shouldn't be in conflict.

For this reason, if you're a religious person and have a relationship with Deity, you should be free to acknowledge that relationship in the basic practices of occultism. That means you can and should include prayer in your daily divination and meditation if you so desire—we have already discussed adding prayer to your divination, and will discuss the role of prayer in meditation in the next chapter—and it also means that in the Sphere of Protection, you can and should call on Deity in whatever way you prefer. The only thing that changes is the wording of the ritual. We'll discuss some of the details in the next section, while dealing with the opening. At the end of this chapter you will find a more complete list of examples, drawn from the experiences of people of many faiths who have practiced the Sphere of Protection.

What if you don't follow any religion? That's not a problem. The basic form of the Sphere of Protection is designed to call on the forces of nature in an impersonal manner. Again, how you invoke spiritual powers in this work is entirely up to you.

Learning the ritual

The Sphere of Protection is best learned a step at a time over an eight week period. Start by learning the Opening and Closing, and practicing just those two for a week. Then add the first of the elemental Callings, the Calling of Air, and practice the Opening, the Calling of Air, and the Closing for a week. Then add in the next of the Callings in its place, and proceed step by step, giving a week to each stage, until you have learned the entire ritual.

One hint that you should keep in mind throughout these instructions: *go back at regular intervals and read the instructions over again*. The human memory is imperfect, and very often you'll find that you've forgotten a detail or gotten something confused. By checking the instructions regularly, it will be easier for you to get the most out of your initiation.

The opening

You perform the Opening of the Sphere of Protection as follows.

* * *

First, stand in the center of your lodge, facing your altar. Take a few moments and a few breaths to focus your attention. Then sweep your arms up to your sides until your hands meet above your head. Put them together as shown, with the fingers of the right hand at right angles across the fingers of the left, as shown in Diagram 3-2. Draw your joined hands down to your forehead, and touch with them the point between your eyebrows, at the location of your third eye center; as you do this, imagine a beam of pure white light descending from infinite space to a point in the center of your head, forming a small sphere of light there. Say the first part of the invocation (to be explained below).

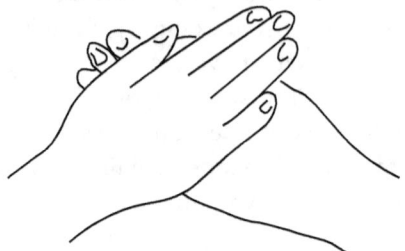

First Position of the Hands.

Second, now draw your joined hands down the front of your body to touch a point on your belly just below your navel, at the location of the womb center. Let your fingers slide against each other so that both sets point down at an angle instead of up, as shown in Diagram 3-3. As you do this, imagine the same beam of pure white light descending through your body to the heart of the Earth. Say the second part of the invocation.

Second Position of the Hands.

Third, now raise your elbows and draw your hands back up, bringing them up and out in a sweeping, blossoming motion. End with your arms out to your sides, palms up. As you do this, imagine the light rising up again from the heart of the Earth, filling your body. Say the third part of the invocation.

Fourth, now cross your arms, right over left, the fingertips of each hand resting against the opposite shoulder. As you do this, imagine the light shining out through your body and filling the space around you, cleansing and blessing all things. Say an appropriate closing phrase This concludes the Opening.

* * *

Let's talk about words. As already noted, what you say will depend on how you want to address the spiritual powers you invoke. The first part of the invocation calls on the principle of Nwyfre, the second part on the principle of Calas, the third on the principle of Gwyar, and the fourth states what you want the opening to do. Here's an example, from the Druid Revival traditions that I follow:

(1) "Hu the Mighty, great Druid god;" (2) "Ced the Earth-mother, source of all life;" (3) "Hesus of the Oaks, chief of tree-spirits;" (4) "May the powers of nature bless and protect me now and always."

Hu the Mighty, Hu Gadarn in Welsh—the name is pronounced "He"—is the sky god of Druid Revival tradition, the master of the stars and the cycles of heaven. Ced—the name is pronounced "Kehd"—is the earth goddess. Hesus or Esus is a tree-god, a child of Hu and Ced, the spirit of the sacred oak and guardian of all Druids. The first is the lord of Nwyfre, the second the lady of Calas, the third the spirit of Gwyar.

Now let's turn to a different tradition—the tradition of Christianity. Here the words used in the Opening are familiar ones to all Christians: (1) "In the name of the Father," (2) "and of the Son," (3) "and of the Holy Spirit," (4) "Amen." You can, if you prefer, simply make the sign of the Cross rather than the gestures given above—the original version of the Sphere of Protection written by Juliet Ashley did exactly this. The three principles are present; God the Father is the lord of Nwyfre, the principle of spirit; God the Son, the Word made Flesh, is the lord of Calas, the principle of substance; and God the Holy Ghost, the rushing wind of Pentecost, is the lord of Gwyar.

For a third example, let's turn to Judaism. The words used by observant Jews who practice this ritual come from the first chapter of the *Sepher Yetzirah*, the oldest work of Jewish Kabbalistic teaching. They are as follows: (1) "One is the Spirit of the Living God." (2) "Blessed and more than blessed be the name of the Living God of Ages." (3) "The Spirit of Holiness is his Voice, his Spirit, and his Word." (4) "Amen."

(If your Hebrew is up to it, by all means use that language instead of English.)

For a fourth example, we can turn to Heathenry, the religion that worships the old Norse and Germanic gods, which has become popular again in North America and many European countries. Here there are several choices, depending on which god or goddess a Heathen has taken for his or her divine patron. One example, though, would be the following: (1) "In the name of Odin," (2) "In the name of Frigga," (3) "And in the name of Balder the Beautiful," (4) "May the blessings of the Aesir and the Vanir be with me now and always."

And if you don't happen to follow the teachings of any religion at this time in your life? The following words are an example of what you can do; they come from the pantheist end of the Druid Revival tradition. (1) "By the sky above me," (2) "by the earth beneath me," (3) "by the life within me," (4) "may I be blessed and renewed now and always."

These examples should give you a good idea of what can be done with the Opening. Whatever the place of religion in your life, there will be some suitable way for you to call on the spiritual powers associated with the three principles.

The closing

The version of the Sphere of Protection devised by John Gilbert included some fairly complicated visualizations, and many students have difficulty with them. For the purpose of this system of training, therefore, I have gone back to Juliet Ashley's simpler version. You'll need to put regular practice into it to make it really effective, though. The Closing is done as follows:

* * *

At the conclusion of the Opening—or, later on, when you have finished all of the elemental Callings—turn your attention to your solar plexus, the area below and behind where the two sides of your ribcage part company. Imagine the beam of pure white light you called down earlier passing through the solar plexus, and forming a small sphere of light there. Feel this as the meeting place of the current of light descending from the sky and the current rising back up from the heart of the Earth.

Now imagine the sphere of light expanding, fed by the two currents flowing into it. It grows until it surrounds your entire body, and as much further as you need to make it to encompass the area you wish to place within its protection. Concentrate, as it expands, on the sense that the space inside it is lighter, cleaner, and brighter than the space outside it. (The more effort you put into this idea, the more effective the ritual will become.)

Pause, once you have expanded the sphere to the size you need it, and feel the space around you as cleansed, lightened, and illuminated. Then cross your arms as you did at the end of the Opening, and say "May the powers of nature bless and protect me this day and always." (You can replace the words "the powers of nature" with a name of Deity if you so wish.) That concludes the closing, and the Sphere of Protection.

* * *

The Opening and Closing are a complete ritual by themselves. Practice them every day for a week, preferably just before doing the first stage of learning discursive meditation (which is discussed in the next section of this book). Take the time to commit each section of the ritual to memory—this is essential. No one ever became good at ritual while they still had to fumble with a book. At the end of the week, you can add the next step—the Calling of Air.

The calling of air

The Opening and Closing are done facing your altar, whichever direction that happens to be. The Calling of Air, on the other hand, is done facing east, the symbolic direction of the element of Air. Before you start this stage of the work, make sure you know which way to turn!

For the second week you spend learning the Sphere of Protection, you will be doing the Opening, the Calling of Air, and the Closing, and by the end of the week, you should be doing all this from memory. Do the ritual as follows:

* * *

First, perform the Opening.

Second, turn to face east (if you're not already facing that way). Using the first two fingers of your right hand, trace the figure in Diagram 3-4 in the air in front of you—first the circle, starting from the top and going clockwise from there, and then the vertical line, from the point where it joins the circle up to the top. Imagine that symbol drawn in a line of yellow flame or blazing yellow light. This is the invoking form of the symbol of air.

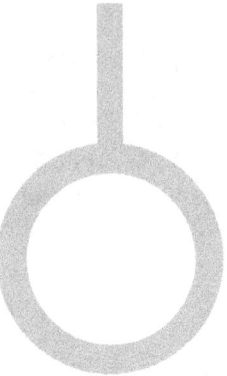

Symbol of Air.

Third, point to the center of the symbol and say these words: "By the yellow gate of the rushing winds and the hawk of May in the heights of morning, I invoke the Air and all its powers. May the powers of Air bless and protect me this day and always, and further my work." (These words and their equivalents in the other elemental Callings can be modified to suit your own spiritual or religious needs, as explained at the end of this chapter.)

Fourth, as you finish the invocation, imagine as intensely as possible a wind blowing out of the east toward you, crisp and fresh. See a morning scene in which the sunrise and the sky dominates all. Make it look like spring in the place where you live. Engage all your senses, so that you smell and feel and hear as well as see the imagery. Breathe the energies of air into yourself. Take a little while at this, and then say, "I thank the powers of Air for their gifts."

Fifth, trace the same symbol in the same place, but this time draw the circle counterclockwise. This is the banishing form of the symbol of Air. It doesn't banish Air—it banishes other things with the help of Air. Point at the center of the circle and say these words: "And with the help of the powers of air, I banish from within me and around me and from all my doings all harmful influences and hostile magic, and every imbalance of the nature of air. I banish these far from me." Spend a little while imagining every imbalance and unwanted influence being swept away by the winds and being lost in the vastness of air.

Sixth, turn to face the same way you faced in the opening, and perform the Closing.

Do this version daily for a week before adding the next element, the Calling of Water.

The calling of water

The Calling of Water is the second of the elemental invocations in the Sphere of Protection ritual. For the third week of this process of initiation, the ritual you'll practice begins wih the Opening and then goes on to the Calling of Air, the Calling of Water, and the Closing, in that order. The symbolic direction of Water is the west, so all you have to do when you finish the Calling of Air is turn around and you'll be facing the right way.

During this week, the Sphere of Protection is practiced as follows:

* * *

First, perform the Opening.

Second, perform the complete Calling of Air, as given above.

Third, turn to face west. Using the first two fingers of your right hand, trace the symbol of Water shown in Diagram 3-5, starting from the bottom point of the triangle and going clockwise. Imagine that symbol drawn, just as shown here, in a line of blue flame or blazing blue light. This is the invoking form of the symbol of water.

Symbol of Water.

Fourth, point to the center of the symbol and say these words: "By the blue gate of the mighty waters and the salmon of wisdom in the sacred pool, I invoke the Water and all its powers. May the powers of Water bless and protect me this day and always, and further my work."

Fifth, as you finish the invocation, imagine as intensely as possible an ocean or a mighty lake reaching out west of you into the distance. See an evening scene in which the sunset shines above the waters. Make it look like autumn in the place where you live. Engage all your senses, so that you smell and feel and hear as well as see the imagery. Draw the energies of water into yourself. Take a little while at this, and then say, "I thank the powers of Water for their gifts."

Sixth, trace the same symbol in the same place, but this time draw the triangle counterclockwise from the bottom. This is the banishing form of the symbol of water. It doesn't banish water—it banishes other things with the help of water. Point at the center of the triangle and say these words: "And with the help of the powers of Water, I banish from within me and around me and from all my doings all harmful influences and hostile magic, and every imbalance of the nature of Water. I banish these far from me." Spend a little while imagining every imbalance and unwanted influence being washed away by the waves and dissolved forever in the vastmess of the water.

Seventh, turn to face the same way you faced in the Opening, and perform the Closing.

Practice this sequence for a week before adding the Calling of Fire.

The calling of fire

By now, you have been practicing the Opening and Closing daily for three weeks, the Calling of Air for two weeks and the Calling of Water for one. Now it's time to add in the third of the elemental phases, the Calling of Fire.

There's a bit of a twist here. You learn the Calling of Water second, but it's not done second once you learn the Calling of Fire. For the next week, you'll be practicing the Opening, the Calling of Air, the Calling of Fire, the Calling of Water, and the Closing, in that order. You'll keep that order, too, when we go on to the remaining four elemental Callings. Why? You need water and air to balance yourself before you invoke fire, but fire goes in the south, so once you've reached this stage, you call fire after air in the east and before water in the west.

During this week, the Sphere of Protection is practiced as follows:

* * *

First, perform the Opening phase of the Sphere of Protection, and then perform the complete Calling of Air, as given above.

Second, face south. Using the first two fingers of your right hand, trace the triangle Diagram 3-6, starting from the top point and going clockwise. Imagine that symbol drawn, just as shown here, in a line of red flame or blazing red light. This is the invoking form of the symbol of fire.

Diagram 3-6.

Third, point to the center of the symbol and say these words: "By the red gate of the bright flames and the white stag of the summer greenwood, I invoke the Fire and all its powers. May the powers of Fire bless and protect me this day and always, and further my work."

Fourth, as you finish the invocation, imagine as intensely as possible the sun blazing high in the southern heavens. See an noonday scene in which heat shimmers in the air. Make it look like summer in the place where you live. Engage all your senses, so that you smell and feel and hear as well as see the imagery. Draw the energies of fire into yourself. Take a little while at this, and then say, "I thank the powers of Fire for their gifts."

Fifth, trace the same symbol in the same place, but this time draw the triangle counterclockwise from the top. This is the banishing form of the symbol of fire. It doesn't banish fire—it banishes other things with the help of fire. Point at the center of the triangle and say these words: "And with the help of the powers of Fire, I banish from within me and around me and from all my doings all harmful influences and hostile magic, and every imbalance of the nature of Fire. I banish these far from me." Spend a little while imagining every imbalance and unwanted influence being shriveled up and burnt away by the heat of the sun.

Sixth, turn to the west, and do the Calling of Water. Finally, face the same way you faced in the Opening, and perform the Closing.

Do this sequence daily for the next week. Notice the change in the energetic balance between this phase and the previous ones.

The calling of earth

This fourth calling is added in the same way as the first three. It goes after the Calling of Water, and is performed facing the north. During the week you spend adding in this Calling, the Sphere of Protection is performned as follows.

* * *

First, perform the Opening phase of the Sphere of Protection, and then perform the complete Callings of Air, Fire, and Water, including both the invoking and the banishing aspects.

Second, face north. Using the first two fingers of your right hand, trace the symbol shown in Diagram 3-7, starting from the point where the circle and line join and going clockwise around the circle, then down the line. Imagine that symbol drawn, just as shown here, in a line of green flame or blazing green light. This is the invoking form of the symbol of earth.

Diagram 3-7.

Third, point to the center of the symbol and say these words: "By the green gate of the tall stones and the great bear of the starry heavens, I invoke the Earth and all its powers. May the powers of Earth bless and protect me this day and always, and further my work."

Fourth, as you finish the invocation, imagine as intensely as possible a night scene lit only by the midnight stars. See the great dim shapes of mountains in the distance. Make it look like winter in the place where you live. Engage all your senses, so that you smell and feel and hear as well as see the imagery. Draw the energies of earth into yourself. Take a little while at this, and then say, "I thank the powers of Earth for their gifts."

Fifth, trace the same symbol in the same place, but this time draw the circle counterclockwise. This is the banishing form of the symbol of earth. It doesn't banish earth—it banishes other things with the help of earth. Point at the center of the symbol and say these words: "And with the help of the powers of Earth, I banish from within me and around me and from all my doings all harmful influences and hostile magic, and every imbalance of the nature of Earth. I banish these far from me." Spend a little while imagining every imbalance and unwanted influence being buried, crushed, and absorbed by the immense quiet weight of earth.

Sixth, face the same way you faced in the Opening, and perform the Closing.

Do this version daily for the next week. Notice the difference in the way the ritual feels now that you have added the element of Earth.

The calling of spirit below

With this week's work, you will bring in the first of the three forms of Spirit invoked in the Sphere of Protection. The Calling of Spirit Below comes after the four Callings you've learned and practiced already, and before the closing. It invokes the telluric current, the great stream of life force that flows upwards from the heart of the earth to bring health and strength to every living thing.

In this Calling, and in the two that follow, you will be invoking but you won't banish. Spirit integrates and harmonizes; you've invoked the four elements to chase off what you need to remove from your life, and now you invoke the three forms of spirit to bring everything else into balance.

During this week, the Sphere of Protection is practiced as follows:

* * *

First, perform the Opening, and then perform the complete Callings of Air, Fire, Water, and Earth.

Second, face the way you did at the opening. Using the first two fingers of your right hand, trace the symbol in Diagram 3-8 as though you were drawing it on the flat surface of a table or altar in front of you. Imagine that symbol drawn in a line of orange flame or blazing orange light. Then imagine it descending a short distance below your feet and moving directly under you. This is the symbol of spirit below.

Diagram 3-8.

Third, point to the center of the symbol and say these words: "By the orange gate of spirit below and the power of the telluric current, I invoke Spirit Below and all its powers. May the powers of Spirit Below bless and protect me this day and always, and further my work."

Fourth, as you finish the invocation, imagine as intensely as possible the deep places of the Earth and the immense powers that dwell there. Engage all your senses, so that you smell and feel and hear as well as see the imagery. Draw the energies of Spirit Below into yourself. Take a little while at this, and then say, "I thank the powers of Spirit Below for their gifts."

Fifth, perform the Closing.

Perform this version of the Sphere of Protection daily for the next week, and notice the difference the presence of Spirit Below makes in the ritual.

The calling of spirit above

This sixth phase of the work invokes the solar current, the great stream of life force that descends from the sun and brings health and strength

THE SPHERE OF PROTECTION   55

to every living thing. It comes after the five Callings you've already learned, and before the Closing.

This version of the Sphere of Protection is done as follows:

* * *

First, perform the Opening and then perform the complete Callings of Air, Fire, Water, Earth, and Spirit Below.

Second, face the same way you did at the opening. Using the first two fingers of your right hand, trace the symbol in Diagram 3-9, as though you were drawing it on a low ceiling over you. Imagine that symbol drawn in a line of purple flame or blazing purple light. Then imagine it ascending a short distance above your head and moving directly over you. This is the symbol of spirit above.

Diagram 3-9.

Third, point up to the center of the symbol and say these words: "By the purple gate of spirit above and the power of the solar current, I invoke Spirit Above and all its powers. May the powers of Spirit Above bless and protect me this day and always, and further my work."

Fourth, as you finish the invocation, imagine as intensely as possible the realms of outer space far above you and the immense powers that dwell there. Engage all your senses, so that you smell and feel and hear as well as see the imagery. (What does outer space smell like? According to astronauts, it smells a little like a scorched barbecue grill—hot metal with an odd hint of meat, due to traces of chemical compounds that drift through the void.) Draw the energies of Spirit Above into yourself. Take a little while at this, and then say, "I thank the powers of Spirit Above for their gifts."

Fifth, perform the Closing.

Perform this version of the Sphere of Protection daily for the next week, and notice the difference the presence of Spirit Above makes in the ritual.

The calling of spirit within

At this point it's time to add in the final elemental phase, the Calling of Spirit Within. This comes after the six Callings you've learned already, and before the Closing. With it, the Sphere of Protection is complete.

In this phase we call on a word of power: Awen, the Grand Word of the Druid tradition. This is pronounced "Aah-Ooo-En," drawn out into three syllables, and it should be spoken in a particular way, which is known as "vibration." To vibrate a word of power is to chant it in a way that sets up a noticeably trembling or tingling in your body.

It's easy to learn to vibrate a word, but a certain amount of practice may be required. Start by practicing with the simple vowel sound "ah." Chant it aloud, and change the way you position your mouth and the way you move your breath until you feel a slight trembling or tingling somewhere in your body. Keep practicing until you can do this whenever you want. Except for this process of learning, you should only vibrate words of power or divine names; it is a sacred way of speaking and should be treated accordingly.

The complete Sphere of Protection, with all seven Callings in place, is performed as follows:

* * *

First, perform the Opening, and then the complete Callings of Air, Fire, Water, Earth, Spirit Below, and Spirit Above.

Second, still facing the same way you did at the opening, visualize all six of the symbols you've traced around yourself, each in its proper color and place, as shown in Diagram 3-10. See yourself in the midst of them. You don't trace a symbol for this Calling because you yourself are the symbol. The powers you are invoking at this stage of the work come from the flame of spirit at the core of yourself.

Then say the following words: "By the six powers here invoked and here present and the secret of the lunar current, and in the Grand Word

AWEN (pronounced Ah-Oo-En), I invoke Spirit Within. May the powers of Spirit Within me bless and protect me this day and always, and further my work. May they establish about me a Sphere of Protection."

The moment you say the words "Sphere of Protection," go immediately to the Closing of the SoP, formulating the sphere around you. This completes the Sphere of Protection.

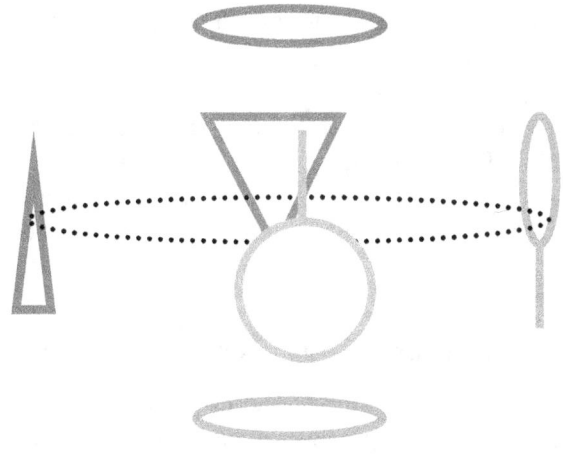

Diagram 3-10.

Understanding the sphere of protection

You can perform the Sphere of Protection or any other ritual by rote and get good results from it. The results will be better still, however, if you understand what you are doing and why. There are two levels to this ritual; you will start with one and gradually, through regular practice, begin to add the other.

The first level works with the relationship between your subjective and objective minds. On this level, the Sphere of Protection works like a series of affirmations given further force by the power of your imagination. In your morning practice, you teach your subjective mind to begin to attune itself to the One Life, and to let the One Life strengthen and sustain you in everything that you do. In the Sphere of Protection, you're doing the same thing in a more powerful and focused way, teaching your subjective mind to attune itself to the different aspects of the One Life one at a time, and to use that attunement to draw in beneficial qualities and to drive off harmful influences. With practice, this becomes an effective way to help your subjective mind take up a more balanced and healthy relationship with life.

The second level goes beyond this, because there's more in the world of the Unseen than your objective and subjective minds! Each of the seven elements invoked in the Sphere of Protection ritual corresponds to a facet of the One Life that exists in the universe, not just in one or both of your minds. By teaching the subjective mind to attune itself to each of these subtle forces, you can literally draw them into yourself, strengthening and empowering yourself with them, and then use them to banish those things you're ready to let go of. As you do this day after day, the effects add up, giving you the power to reshape your life in constructive ways. The Sphere of Protection won't bring results instantly, but over time you'll be astonished by the benefits it will bring to you.

Divine names and the sphere of protection

As mentioned earlier, if you have religious beliefs, you may certainly make them part of your practice of the Sphere of Protection. Occultism isn't a religion and it doesn't conflict with religion. If you have a relationship with a deity or deities, it's appropriate for you to include prayer and religious invocation in your occult work if you feel called to do so.

The section above on the Opening of the Sphere of Protection describes one way in which you can include your religious beliefs in this practice. If you want to go further, you can invoke a divine name in each of the six quarters to add strength to the working. This is done by adding a section to each of the invocations. For example, when I perform the first calling, drawing on my Druid faith, I say, "By the yellow gate of the rushing winds and the hawk of May in the heights of morning, and in the great name Hu, I invoke the Air…" and so on. You can substitute any appropriate name or phrase for "the great name Hu."

People of many different religions have practiced the Sphere of Protection and adapted the ritual to call on the names of the spiritual powers they revere. Here is a selection of those religious adaptations of the Sphere of Protection that I know of:

Christian (Catholic)

East: St. Matthew
West: St. John
South: St. Mark
North: St. Luke
Below: your own patron saint
Above: the Blessed Virgin Mary
With each of these, after saying "I thank the powers of (element) for their gifts," say, "Blessed St. (name), pray for me."

Christian (Protestant)

In many Protestant denominations it is traditional to call only on the name of Jesus, "the name that is above all other names." Fortunately Jesus has many titles in the Bible, and these can be used in the ritual as follows. In using these, say, "… and in the name of Jesus, the Word" and so on. (I have included scriptural references for the curious.)
East: the Word (John 1:1)
West: Emmanuel (Isaiah 7:14)
South: the Sun of Righteousness (Malachi 4:2)
North: the Son of David (Matthew 1:1)
Below: the Good Shepherd (John 10:11)
Above: the Resurrection and the Life (John 11:25)

Druid (Irish)

East: Aengus the god of love and youth
West: Manannan the sea god
South: Brigid the goddess of poetry, healing, and smithcraft
North: Aine the goddess of sovereignty
Below: Danu the earth goddess
Above: Dagda the king of the gods

Druid (Welsh)

East: Hu the Mighty, the great Druid god
West: Hesus of the Oaks, chief of tree-spirits

South: Sul of the sun and the healing springs
North: Elen of the Roads, goddess of dawn and dusk
Below: Cêd the Earth Mother, source of all life
Above: Celi the Hidden One

Egyptian Pagan

East: Horus the hawk-headed god
West: Anubis the jackal-headed god
South: Isis the bright goddess
North: Nephthys the dark goddess
Below: Osiris the Lord of the Dead
Above: Ra the sun god

Esoteric Buddhist

This set is derived from Shingon Buddhism, one of the two main Japanese esoteric Buddhist sects. I have given both the Sanskrit and the Japanese names of the Buddhas. The Opening that goes with this set invokes the Three Refuges: (1) "I take refuge in the Buddha." (2) "I take refuge in the Dharma." (3) "I take refuge in the Sangha." (4) "OM."

East Aksobhya/Ashuku, the Buddha of Humility
West: Amitabha/Amida Nyorai, the Buddha of Compassion
South: Ratnasambhava/Hosho Nyorai, the Buddha of Generosity
North: Amoghasiddhi/Fukujoju Nyorai, the Buddha of Fearlessness
Below: Sakyamuni/Shaka Nyorai, the historical Buddha
Above: Vairocana/Dainichi Nyorai, the Great Sun Buddha

Heathen (Anglo-Saxon)

East: Woden the god of wisdom
West: Frig the goddess of bounty
South: Thunor the thunder god
North: Ing the god of fertility
Below: Erce the earth goddess
Above: Tiw the sky god

Heathen (Norse)

East: Thor the thunder and storm god
West: Frey the god of fertility and abundance
South: Freyja the queen of the Valkyries and warrior goddess
North: Idun the keeper of the apples of immortality
Below: Frigga the queen of the Aesir and spinner of fates
Above: Odin, seated on Hlidskjalf at the summit of the worlds

Hellenic (Greek Pagan)

East: Athena the goddess of wisdom and civilization
West: Aphrodite the sea-born goddess of love and fertility
South: Apollo the sun god and lord of light
North: Dionysus the master of animals
Below: Demeter the goddess of soil and grain
Above: Zeus the lord of wind and lightning

Hindu

The Hindu faith assigns gods to the directions, and the Sphere of Protection thus works well within a Hindu context. The *lokapalas* or guardians of the directions can be visualized on their traditional animal vehicles, and with their consorts.

East: Indra, god of the storm
West: Varuna, god of the oceans
South: Yama, god of justice
North: Kubera, god of wealth
Below: Vishnu the Preserver
Above: Brahma the Creator

Jewish

The *Sepher Yetzirah*, the most ancient volume of Jewish Cabalistic teaching, assigns divine names of three letters each to the six directions of space. (The passage where it does this is chapter 1, verse 11.) Applied to the Sphere of Protection, they are as follows:

East: ויה (Heh Yod Vau).
West: יהו (Vau Heh Yod).
South: היו (Vau Yod Heh).
North: יוה (Heh Vau Yod).
Below: הוי (Yod Vau Heh).
Above: והי (Yod Heh Vau).

It's traditional to pronounce these by using the names of the letters. "By the yellow gate of the rushing winds and the hawk of May in the heights of morning, and in the Great Name Heh Yod Vau..." is an example.

Roman Pagan

Rome had its own pantheon in the days before Greek culture and religion were adopted by many educated Romans. Many of today's Roman Pagans have gone back to that older pantheon, and the list below follows that approach.

East: Mavors/Mars the warrior god
West: Neptune the sea god
South: Vesta the hearth goddess
North: Ceres the earth goddess
Below: Veiovis the underworld god of wealth
Above: Jupiter the sky god

CHAPTER FOUR

Meditation and scrying

The second of the major practices in the Golden Section Fellowship is meditation—a specific kind of meditation with deep roots in Western culture. Many people these days are surprised to learn that there are any traditions of Western meditation at all. Since the latter years of the nineteenth century, when the Theosophical Society first introduced Eastern meditation to the Western world, quite a few people in Europe and America have had a hard time thinking of meditation at all without conjuring up images of yogis in orange robes chanting mantras on the banks of the Ganges, Zen monks in black kimonos sitting in lotus posture in the severe elegance of a Japanese monastery, or similar notions freighted with exotic imagery.

Yet meditation has an equally long pedigree in the West, reaching back through ancient Greece to the temple disciplines of Egypt. Until the industrial revolution, most religious people in Europe practiced it as a matter of course. The word "meditation" itself didn't have to be imported from the East, for that matter. It comes from Latin, and *meditatio* in that language has referred to what we now call meditation for many centuries.

The Latin word *meditatio* doesn't just refer to meditation, though. It also means thinking, and focused, deliberate thinking in particular.

Other English words derived from the same root contain this second meaning. When prosecutors file charges of premeditated murder, for example, they don't mean that the criminal chanted a mantra or silenced his mind before committing the crime; it means that the criminal thought it through, planned it, and deliberately decided to do it.

This points to a core difference between Eastern and Western methods of meditation, one that has already been mentioned in an earlier chapter. Although there are exceptions, most Eastern methods of meditation work by turning off the objective mind. In some of these kinds of meditation, students learn to fix the attention on something other than thinking—a repeated mantra, a visualization, a cycle of breathing, or bare attention itself—so that their objective minds stop thinking altogether, and deeper patterns of awareness come to the fore. Others do the same thing in a subtler way, by teaching students to observe thoughts rising in the objective mind without actually thinking about them. Either of these can result in powerful spiritual experiences, but they have significant drawbacks. Shutting down the objective mind in this way too often produces people who have experienced deep spiritual states but have never learned how to think clearly, and often can't function well in everyday life.

The core traditions of Western meditation take a different path. Instead of stopping the thinking process, these methods point the focus of the objective mind on thinking itself, and turn the objective mind into a vehicle for spiritual awareness. In the standard Western method of meditation, this is done by focusing the mind on a specific topic, called a *theme*, and mentally following out the implications of that theme through a chain of ideas, all the while keeping the objective mind focused on the theme. With practice, the subjective mind joins in, and begins to hand the objective mind ideas and insights it wouldn't otherwise have had, so that meditation becomes another way for your two minds to work together.

This form of meditation is called *discursive meditation*, because it often takes the form of an inner discourse or dialogue. Discursive meditation has all the benefits that other methods of meditation yield—relaxation, serenity, spiritual development, the the like—but it also has two other benefits that most other methods of meditation don't. First, given time and practice, it gradually transforms thinking from half-random mental chatter into a powerful and focused way of understanding that can be used for many purposes. In this way the objective mind becomes an ally, not an enemy, of the spiritual path.

The second benefit is even more important for the occultist. For countless centuries, spiritual teachings have been woven into symbols and images in ways that are far from obvious. This was partly a way of keeping the teachings and their students safe during the bitter years of persecution, but it has another side that remains important even in an age of liberty. There are things that cannot be communicated in ordinary language, but can be passed on by way of carefully designed symbols that are explored in meditation. The higher states of consciousness and many of the realities experienced in those states are among these things—and for this reason, symbolic images have long been used to pass on these otherwise incommunicable realities. To learn discursive meditation is to take up the key that alone can unlock the deeper dimensions of sacred geometry, the images of the tarot, the emblems of the alchemists, and much more.

Until a little more than a century ago, for these reasons, discursive meditation used to be a common practice all across the Western world. It was taught by many churches and other religious organizations as well as in secular settings. In the occult schools of the Western world, discursive meditation was one of the core practices taught to initiates, and it was combined with another form of practice called scrying or active imagination. Both discursive meditation and scrying are core practices of the Golden Section Fellowship, and you should plan on learning and practicing them as you prepare for your initiation.

The art of discursive meditation

If you've practiced other kinds of meditation, discursive meditation will seem partly familiar to you and partly strange. If you've never meditated, the entire process will probably seem very strange to you! For that reason, it's best to learn discursive meditation a step at a time, beginning with posture. You'll be doing all of the following steps in your lodge, sitting on the chair facing the altar. If you can place a clock where you can see it without turning your head, that will be very helpful.

One final tip: if your schedule permits, always do your meditation right after performing the Sphere of Protection ritual. You can set up your chair facing the altar, perform the Sphere of Protection, then sit down in the chair at once and go straight into meditation from there. This makes meditation easier and more effective, since when you finish the ritual, your objective and subjective minds will both be a little more balanced and a little better attuned to the One Life.

Posture

One of the benefits of discursive meditation is that you don't have to tie your legs into a knot to practice it, and in fact it's not helpful to do that. The posture to use is the one shown in any Egyptian statue of a seated god or goddess. Sit on a relatively hard chair. If it has a back, slide forward, so your back doesn't touch the chair's back at all. (This allows subtle energies to flow freely up and down your spine, which makes meditation easier.) Your feet should rest flat on the floor, your knees and hips are at right angles, your hands rest palm down on your thighs, and your head is straight. Keep your eyes open but relax your eyelids; took forward and down, as though at something on the floor a few yards ahead of you. Breathe slowly and easily.

When you're ready to practice, take this position, and don't move for five minutes. Don't fidget, shift, wiggle, scratch an itch or anything else. Leave your body completely still for five minutes by the clock. Do this once a day, preferably first thing in the morning, after your morning practice but before breakfast. That's your assignment for the first week.

Unless you've already done this, or practiced certain other exercises that have the same effect, this is going to be much harder than you think. Our bodies are actually full of tensions and discomforts we never notice, and part of the constant shifting and wiggling and fidgeting that most of us do most of the time is a matter of trying not to notice just how uncomfortable we are. Confront that evasion head on. Stay still for those five minutes, no matter what.

If you do that, you'll begin to learn one of the essential secrets of meditation. It is literally the most boring, grueling, frustrating thing you will ever do—and once you get the hang of how to do it and why it's important, you'll do it every day, because the payoffs are worth so much more than the boredom.

Relaxation

Thie second week's work is also on the material plane, and focused on relaxation. Most people these days realize that it's possible to be too tense. Since the opposite of one bad idea is generally another bad idea, it's worth remembering that it's also possible to be too relaxed. Until very recently, most people in Western societies were much too tense.

It was extremely rare to encounter anyone in the Western world who was too relaxed, whose body was so lacking in tension that it was limp and floppy, and so teachers of spiritual exercises put a lot of focus into relaxation. That had its effect, and now you find people on either end of the spectrum. What you find too rarely is people who have the balanced midpoint between too much tension and too much relaxation, which we can call poise.

The practice of sitting in a fixed and slightly unnatural posture is meant to keep you from being too relaxed. Keeping the spine straight, the head held up, the legs parallel, and the body still requires tension. Now we move to the other side of the balance and make sure you aren't too tense. This is done by relaxing your muscles while retaining the posture you've established. You don't move at all; you don't shift or wiggle or stretch; you just let go of the tensions you don't need to keep the posture.

Here's how it's done. Start at the crown of the head. Consciously relax any muscular tensions you find there. If you encounter a tension that won't let go, imagine that it is relaxing. (Your subjective mind will notice this, and the imagination will become reality with a little practice.) Spend a little while on that part of your body, and then move further down your head to the sides of the skull. Consciously relax any tensions you find there, if you can, and if you can't, imagine the tensions dissolving. Go all the way down your whole body this way, taking it a bit at a time, and doing the same twofold relaxation on each part of your body—consciously relax what you can, and imagine the rest letting go. This should take you at least five minutes, and quite possibly more than that. All the while, maintain the seated posture without moving. Don't pay attention to your breath—that's a later phase—or to anything outside yourself; simply focus on your body, and on the process by which you're releasing unnecessary tensions.

You may find that when you finish this, you ache from head to foot, or that some part of your body hurts a little—or a lot. That's what happens when you have a lot of unnecessary tension you stopped noticing a long time ago. With repeated practice, the tension will go away. You may also find that when you finish this, some of your muscles feel as though they've had a workout. They have—you've been holding your body in an unfamiliar position for a while, and that takes muscular effort. Your body will get used to that in due time.

That's the second stage of preparation for meditation: five minutes a day, sitting motionless in a chair, relaxing your unnecessary tensions. Do this for a week before going on to the next stage.

Breathing

How you breathe has powerful effects on your state of consciousness, and there are intricate systems of breathwork that take advantage of this for various purposes. If you don't have a teacher to supervise you and watch for signs of trouble, though, those can be risky. Breathwork stimulates the vagus nerve, a nerve that connects the vital organs with the brain, and so has a range of effects on your nervous system and your glands; if you do intensive breathwork without supervision, you can mess up your health.

Fortunately there are methods of breathwork that are safe to practice on your own, and one of them is very commonly used in discursive meditation practice. It's called the Fourfold Breath. It's quite simple. You breathe in through your nose, slowly and deeply, to the count of four. You hold the breath in to the count of four. You breathe out through your nose, slowly and fully, to the count of four. You hold the breath out to the count of four. Repeat to the same steady rhythm.

How do you know how slow or fast to make the rhythm? Simply make it reasonably slow, but not so slow that you gasp or run out of air. Keep the movement of your breath steady, gentle, and flowing. No two people will have exactly the same rhythm, nor will you have the same rhythm every time you practice. Don't use a metronome or any other mechanical aid; just let yourself find a pace that works for you.

One detail worth noting is that you don't hold your breath by closing your throat; you hold it by keeping the muscles of your chest and abdomen in their positions, either expanded or relaxed. If you're used to closing your throat to hold your breath, it can take some practice to stop doing so. How do you tell if you're closing your throat? Draw in a deep breath, hold it for a little while, and then breathe out. If you hear or feel a little "pop" inside your throat, you've closed it. To keep from doing that, keep trying to breathe in a trickle of air while you hold your breath in, and keep trying to breathe out a trickle of air when you're holding your breath out. You'll get the hang of it quickly.

For the next week, five minutes of the Fourfold Breath will be your practice. Take the position, hold yourself still, and let the tension drain away from the crown of your head to the soles of your feet, just as you did last week. Take a minute or two to do this, then begin the Fourfold Breath. Keep doing it for five minutes by the clock. This is the sequence you'll use to begin the process of meditation for real next week. Keep at it, and see where it take you.

Meditation

So far we've dealt with posture, relaxation, and breathing: the preliminaries to discursive meditation. Now it's time to go all the way and meditate. To make sense of what follows, it's important to remember that the word "meditation" literally means "thinking." As noted earlier, when you say that a crime was premeditated, you don't mean that the perpetrator did it in a blissed-out state with an empty mind. You mean he thought deliberately, seriously, and intentionally about the crime before he did it. So that's what you're going to do—no, not commit a crime, but think deliberately, seriously, and intentionally about something. In a moment, we'll talk about how to choose a theme for your meditation; for now, let's focus on the technique of meditation itself.

When you're ready to begin meditation, sit down in the position we've discussed and settle into it, neither tense nor relaxed but poised. Let go of excess tension, beginning from the top of your head and letting it drain down from there; spend about a minute at that. Then do five minutes of the Fourfold Breath, letting your mind focus solely on your breathing. Then you're ready to begin. Call to mind the theme on which you're going to meditate. If the theme is a sentence or a phrase, repeat it silently to yourself several times. If it's an image, see it as clearly as possible in your mind's eye. In either case, hold it in your mind for a little while, and then begin thinking about it.

As you do so, your thoughts will wander off the theme. Bring them back. They'll wander off again. Bring them back again. You'll have as much trouble keeping your mind on the theme as the practitioner of mind-emptying styles of meditation has keeping thoughts at bay, and you'll develop the same skills of catching your mind wandering and bringing it back to the subject of the meditation. In the intervals between these vagaries, on the other hand, you'll be learning something about the theme, and you'll also be working on the capacity for focused reflective thought, an essential human skill and one very poorly developed by most of us. Keep working on the theme for ten minutes by the clock.

In order to practice this kind of focused thinking, of course, you need something to think about. The subject for a discursive meditation is known as the *theme*. You can use anything as a theme that you want to understand. Remember that you can combine your meditation with your evening practice by choosing a theme each night, having it in your mind when you go to bed, and then meditating on it in the morning!

It's standard practice to choose themes from whatever spiritual path you follow, and some paths have specific bodies of lore that are typically used for discursive meditation. In the Golden Section Fellowship, the first set of themes to use for your meditations comes from the Sacred Geometry Oracle. Each card in the Oracle has a meditation that goes with it, and you should plan on completing the whole sequence, devoting one day to each card. These thirty-three sessions of meditation—just over a month of daily practice—are a core part of your preparation for initiation into the Golden Section Fellowship and should not be neglected or scanted.

And after that? As of this writing I am working on one book, *The Occult Philosophy Workbook*, which gives themes for one year of daily meditations, and several others are in preparation. As an initiate of the Golden Section Fellowship, however, you are free to meditate on whatever subjects interest you, whether or not they are covered in books issued for the Fellowship's use. Broadly speaking, there are two sources of themes for meditation you will find useful—written texts and images. Examples of the first kind include classic texts of occult teaching such as Eliphas Lévi's *The Doctrine and Ritual of High Magic* and Dion Fortune's *The Mystical Qabalah*, or important spiritual texts such as the *Tao Te Ching* and the Gospel according to John. Examples of the second kind include the imagery of the tarot trumps, the mystic diagrams of the alchemists, and the tracing boards of the degrees of Freemasonry.

Whether you want to work with texts or images, the key to choosing a theme for meditation is to take it in little bites. If you are meditating on a written text, take it one sentence at a time, or even a phrase at a time. If you've chosen to meditate on the Gospel according to John, for example, you might start with the first phrase: "In the beginning was the Word." Ask yourself questions about that: what is a word? Why is Christ described as a Word? A word implies a speaker and a listener; who speaks the Word, and who hears it? What does the Word mean? Questions like these will make for a rich meditation.

Similarly, if you are meditating on an image, take it one detail at a time. If you've chosen to meditate on the tarot trumps, for example, you might start with the first card, the Fool. Don't try to absorb all of it at once; take one detail at a time, giving each detail its own session of meditation. Say you decide to meditate on the dog who follows barking after the Fool. Ask yourself questions about the dog: why is there a dog in the card? What might it symbolize? What is it doing? How does it relate to the other things in the card—the fool himself, the cliff, the mountains, the sun? What message might it be meant to communicate?

As you practice meditation, you'll learn what kinds of questions help you unfold the secrets of a text or an image, and you'll also learn what kinds of texts and images make good raw material for discursive meditation. Learn from your experiences and choose new themes accordingly. To become a member of the Fellowship is to commit yourself to the quest for wisdom, but only you can decide where that quest will lead you.

Prayer

If you are a religious person, it's traditional to add prayer to discursive meditation. There are two standard ways to do this, and you may do either one, both, or none at all, depending on your personal preferences.

The first way is to say a short prayer just after you finish the fourfold breath and just before you begin the meditation itself. Here you are asking Deity for help with the work of meditation, as you would ask for help in any other part of your life. This doesn't have to be complex and it certainly shouldn't be lengthy. One example, from my own faith tradition, is as follows: "Hu the Mighty, great Druid god, enlighten me through thy initiation." You can use something suitable from your own faith, or come up with words of your own.

The second way is to let your meditation end in prayer. Here spontaneous prayer is more appropriate. Once you've finished exploring the theme of the meditation, turn your attention toward Deity and begin to pray. Very often, once you get into the habit of doing this, you will find that the theme of the meditation will suggest to you subjects for prayer. The prayer can be as long or short as you wish it to be; simply make it a habit to talk to Deity at the end of each session of meditation.

Whichever of these you do, always remember to follow the prayer with a short period of silence. Too many people who pray forget that a prayer is a conversation, and to have a conversation you need to leave room for the other person to talk! When you finish talking, listen inwardly; you may not get a response, especially at first—or, more to the point, you may not be aware of the response you get. Answers to prayer are rarely in words, and it can take time and practice to learn to sense the other side of the conversation.

What if you don't feel comfortable adding prayer to your meditations? Then don't do it. This side of the practice is optional, not mandatory. Many religious people find that meditation with prayer gets better results than without, but if for any reason you don't feel that this is appropriate for you, set it aside and do your meditations as already outlined.

Closing self-massage

When you finish meditating, it's helpful to do something to bring your attention back to ordinary concerns so you can go on with your day. Druids in Brittany and France many years ago took up a set of simple self-massage movements that do this very effectively. The movements come from Do-In (pronounced dough-inn), one of the most ancient of the Asian healing arts, and they are easy to learn and practice. They focus on the hands, head, and feet, since these are where most of the subtle channels of the One Life in the body begin and end.

The sequence recommended after each session of discursive meditation is very simple and takes just a few minutes. You do it sitting in your chair right after you finish meditating.

There's a crucial detail to this practice that beginners too often forget, however, so I'm going to put it here and then repeat it. *Between each exercise, pause, breathe deeply, and relax.* Imagine tension draining out of you. That moment of stillness is as important, if not more so, than the exercise itself.

First, rub your hands together vigorously, palm to palm. Then rub the back of each hand and fingers with the other hand. Do this until the skin is warm.

Now pause, breathe, and relax.

Second, hold your arms out loosely in front of you and shake your hands, letting them flop freely. Do this for a minute or so.

Now pause, breathe, and relax.

Third, wrap the fingers of one hand around the thumb of the other, as though taking hold of a handle. Pull gently, and let your thumb slide out against the pressure of the fingers. Do this to every finger on both hands in turn.

Now pause, breathe, and relax.

Fourth, rub your face, making little circles with your fingertips. Start up at the hairline (or where your hairline used to be, if you're balding) and work down the face, trying not to miss any spot. Press harder or softer depending on how it feels—if it hurts, you're pressing too hard.

Now pause, breathe, and relax.

Fifth, form your hands into loose fists, and tap them gently and rhythmically all over your scalp, from your hairline back and around all the way to the nape of your neck and from one side to the other. Again, if it hurts you're doing it too hard.

Now pause, breathe, and relax.

Sixth, still sitting, cross one leg across the other knee, so it's easy for you to get to your foot. Tap the sole of your foot from the heel up to the toes with a loose fist. Most people can do this a good deal harder here than on the scalp! Then, using both hands, rub the top and sole of the foot until the skin is warm. (You can do this in stocking feet if you prefer—it's just as effective.)

Put your foot down flat. Now pause, breathe, and relax.

Seventh, repeat the process with your other foot.

Put that foot down flat. Now pause, breathe, and relax.

That completes the process. If you like, and have access to a book or website on Do-In, you can do more than this basic sequence. As explained a littler later on, each member of the Fellowship is encouraged to take up a body-oriented practice alongside the other practices taught in this book, and Do-In is certainly one of the possibilities

Going further with meditation

At this point you've covered all the steps involved in discursive meditation: choose a theme; settle your physical body; let go of unhelpful tensions; use rhythmic breathing to settle your etheric and astral bodies; think, slowly, patiently, with as much mental focus as you can manage, about the theme of your choice; and close with self-massage. That's the entire method. If you know that much and practice it daily, you'll go step by step through the learning curve of discursive meditation and achieve the states of increased clarity, perception, and wisdom that meditation brings. Yes, it really is that simple.

Are there difficulties? Of course. I've already mentioned that meditation is the most boring activity you will ever experience, and I mean that quite literally. At some points it's maddeningly dull. That's true of every kind of meditation, by the way, and it's essential to its effectiveness. Boredom is always a sign that you're not paying enough attention. Meditation works by teaching you to notice what you don't usually notice, to pay attention to the things that usually slide right past you. Thus there are two rules for dealing with boredom in meditation. The first is to keep going; the second is to slow down and pay more attention. That's not easy, but it'll get you through the boredom and help you notice what you've been missing.

You'll almost certainly go through the stage at which your body itches, aches, and throws every other possible annoying and distracting physical sensation at you. All those are sensations that you've been having all along anyway, without noticing them. Now that you're quieting the constant babble of sensory and mental chatter, you're going to notice them. Remain motionless and keep on with the meditation; you can scratch or whatever once your meditation session is over. This is a passing phase and your body will quiet back down after a while.

Many people also go through a stage when, as soon as they start meditation, they get really sleepy. That's another body issue. Sometimes it's a way for your body to tell you that you aren't getting enough sleep, and sometimes your body simply isn't used to being quiet except when you're going to sleep, and so it treats the meditation session as the lead-in to a nap. Fairly often this is just another passing phase. If it's not, you can add a bit of physical discomfort into the mix. (I had a hard time with this early on in my practice, and solved it by meditating stark naked on a folding metal chair—oh, and did I mention that it was winter? The cold kept me from feeling drowsy, and that got my body out of the habit of treating meditation as naptime.)

Some other points may be worth mentioning. Most people find that it helps to meditate at the same time every day, so that it becomes a habit. Most people find that it's a good idea to wait at least an hour after eating a meal or having sex before practicing meditation—in both cases, your body has most of its energies directed somewhere other than the thinking centers in the head, and needs time to redirect those.

Traditional lore has it that it's a bad idea to meditate while drunk or under the influence of drugs, though a mild dose of caffeine seems to be exempt from that—Zen monks in Japan drink green tea before meditating, and so do I, with good results.

Finally, there's a habit you may want to try introducing into your practice once you've gotten some experience with discursive meditation. When you're meditating and realize that your mind has gone running off after something other than the theme of your meditation, don't just pop it right back onto the theme. Instead, notice what it's thinking about, and then work your way back through the chain of associations that got it to where it was. If you suddenly notice that you're thinking about your grandmother, let's say, stop there and go back. Why were you thinking about your grandmother? Because you were remembering a Thanksgiving dinner at her house when you were a child. Why did that memory come to mind? Because you were thinking about nuts, and she always had bowls of mixed nuts out on Thanksgiving day. Why were you thinking about nuts? Because you thought about squirrels, and the association came to mind. Why were you thinking about squirrels? Because one ran across the roof of your house, and the skittering noise broke into your train of thought and distracted you from your theme.

Trace the distracting thoughts back to their origins over and over again, and you'll find that it trains your mind to run back to the theme just as readily as it ran away from it. You'll also become more aware of your habitual thought patterns, which is a serious benefit, as this will teach you over time to work with them consciously rather than having them control you unconsciously. Give it a try and see where it takes you.

The art of scrying

In Western occult teachings generally, and in the work of the Golden Section Fellowship in particular, discursive meditation is paired with another meditative exercise, which is called scrying. Scrying originally meant seeing in the ordinary sense—the word "descry," meaning "to see something at a distance," still gets a little use in poetry and literature—but the word was adopted centuries ago by occultists for a very special kind of seeing that doesn't rely on the physical eyes.

To understand scrying, it helps to know a little about the part of the Unseen that occultists call the astral plane. This is the realm of dreams and visions, and also of most ordinary kinds of thinking. Most of the time, when you have an experience that doesn't come through your physical senses but resembles something that does—when you see something in your mind's eye, hear something that is said to you in a dream, remember the flavor of something you used to enjoy in childhood, or anything of that kind—you're perceiving something on the astral plane.

One of the things that makes the astral plane tricky, especially at first, is that some of the things you experience in your imagination, your dreams, your memories, and your ordinary thoughts seem to come from your objective mind. Remember the straightedge that you imagined while reading Chapter One? That's a good example. Other things, though, show up without your objective mind having anything to do with the matter. It's as though you were looking at a movie screen with two projectors pointed at it. Your objective mind runs one of the projectors, but the other one is controlled by your subjective mind, and the films it shows you are chosen partly from the subjective mind's own thoughts and memories, and partly from the unseen world outside both of your two minds.

One further thing to remember about the astral plane is that it works by association. What does that mean? It means that if you call one image to mind, other images that are associated with it will tend to follow it into your thoughts. Some of these associations are in your own thoughts and memories—think of the example given earlier, in which a squirrel was associated with nuts, nuts with Thanksgiving dinner, and Thanksgiving dinner with your grandmother. Some of the associations, however, reach out into the Unseen, connecting with things outside your two minds, and learning how to tap into those connections and make contact with associations that don't come from your own thoughts and memories is an important occult skill. Scrying is one of the safest and most effective ways to do that, and it has been used for several centuries now among occultists.

Scrying works with your imagination in much the same way that discursive meditation works with your thoughts. To scry, you start with a *portal image*, which serves the same function as the theme does in discursive meditation. A portal image combines two symbols—the first is a symbol that lets your subjective mind know you're turning your attention to associations on the astral plane, the second is the specific symbol you want to use to draw associations to you. Standard occult practice for many years has been to use the image of a doorway for the first, and to put the second symbol on the doorway as though it's painted or carved there.

You use the same posture and preliminary steps for scrying that you use for meditation. Sit down in the posture, relax your material body from head to toe, and spend five minutes doing the Fourfold Breath. If you pray at this point in your meditation, do exactly the same thing when scrying. Once you're ready, imagine the portal image in front of you: a door with the symbol you've chosen painted or carved on it. Imagine that your altar isn't there—the portal image is there instead, a door to unknown realms.

(It's probably a good idea to repeat here a point made earlier in this book: if your imagination doesn't give you the kind of images you'd expect on a movie screen or in a video game, that doesn't matter. Always bring in all the imaginary senses, not just sight: imagine how the door feels and sounds and smells, as well as how it looks, and if all you can do is know that the portal image is there, that's good enough. As with everything else you do, you'll get better at this with practice.)

Once you've built up the portal image as clearly as you can, imagine the door swinging slowly open. Beyond it is a landscape of some sort. Don't decide what it looks like in advance. Let it be whatever comes into your mind, and spend a minute or more letting it take shape in your imagination before going on. Then, slowly and clearly, imagine yourself getting up out of your chair, walking up to the doorway, and going through it. The door remains open behind you, and if you look back you can see your physical body sitting in the chair in your lodge. Look around at the realm beyond the door, and notice as many details as you can.

For your first few experiments in scrying, this is as much as you need to do. Once you're familiar with the practice you can go further. The best way to do this is to call for a guide. As you stand there in the imaginary landscape beyond the door, imagine yourself saying aloud, "In the name of the Eternal Spiritual Sun I ask that a true and faithful guide be sent to me." (If you are a religious person you can use a name of Deity in place of the reference to the Eternal Spiritual Sun.) Then, imagine a guide coming to you. Don't decide in advance who or what the guide will be. Let it be whatever appears in your imagination at that moment. It may take human, animal, or some other form.

Whatever its form, ask it whether it comes in the name of the Eternal Spiritual Sun (or the name of Deity if you've used that instead.) Talk with it, and ask it to show you some of the secrets of whatever symbol it is you put into the portal image. Your guide will most likely take you on a journey through the imaginary landscape beyond the portal image, showing you things that reveal something of the inner meaning of the symbol, and it may also instruct you directly. Ask it any questions you wish, and pay close attention to its answers. Every detail of the landscape around you and every word spoken to you has something to teach. Treat the things you encounter as though they were real, for as long as the scrying lasts.

A certain degree of caution is in order when dealing with the guide and the other beings you may encounter in the imaginary space beyond the portal image. Some of these are honest and will teach you worthwhile things, but others may try to deceive you. Some people find it hard to think of imaginary beings in these terms, but the metaphor of the screen with two projectors should be kept in mind here. Imaginary beings can be as independent of the scryer's will as the people who appear in dreams; they have a life of their own, and can behave in unexpected ways. Treat them with the same courtesy and caution you would use toward strangers in an unfamiliar town.

When the journey or the instruction comes to an end, ask your guide to bring you back to your starting point, thank it for its guidance and bless it in the name of the Eternal Spiritual Sun or the name of Deity you invoked earlier. Then return through the doorway, imagine yourself sitting back in the chair where your physical body has been all the while, and then slowly and carefully imagine the door closing. As it closes, concentrate on the thought that no unwanted energies or beings can come into your daily life from the realm you've been scrying. Use a few cycles of fourfold breath to clear your mind, then close just as you would at the end of a session of meditation, complete with self-massage. Write up the experience in your practice journal as soon as possible, while the details are still fresh in your mind.

You may find yourself a little disoriented at first after scrying, especially the first few times you do it. If so, eating some food will help refocus your attention on your body and the material plane of existence. Routine activities such as washing the dishes can also help reorient your awareness back to the realm of ordinary experience.

Working with scrying

As already noted, scrying is a kind of meditation that works with your imagination rather than your thoughts. Once you've become comfortable with discursive meditation, you can start using scrying now and then in place of your regular discursive meditation. The images and ideas you get from your scrying then become themes for discursive meditations in the days that follow. For every day you practice scrying, plan on spending at least three days, and maybe more, using discursive meditation to make sense of the meaning of the things you saw and heard during the scrying. For example, you can look back over the entry in your practice journal and sort out what you encountered into events, symbols, and information, and then devote one session of meditiation to each of these.

An example may help here. Suppose you practiced scrying using the twelfth card of the Sacred Geometry Oracle, The Square, as the symbol on your portal image. You go through the portal in your imagination, and find yourself in a meadow at sunset surrounded by trees. You call for a guide, and an old woman in a green robe approaches you. She leads you to the center of the meadow. There, by the fading daylight, you see a stone sunk in the ground. It is square, and carved into it is the image of a man and a woman holding hands. Once the scrying is over, you write down everything you experienced during it, and then over the next few days you meditate on them.

What did it mean that you were in a meadow? Why was it at sunset? Why was your guide an old woman, and what did it mean that she wore a green robe? Why was there a stone at the center of the circle, why was it square, and what did the image of the man and the woman mean? As you explore these and similar questions, remember that there are no right answers and no wrong answers. The goal of this exercise is not to come up with some set of standardized result, but to teach your objective mind to be attentive to symbols, to think with them, to get a sense of the things they can mean and the things they mean to you personally. Feel free, when meditating on the results of a scrying, to draw on your own memories and inner life as a resource. Does the meadow you say while scrying remind you of a place you visited in childhood, for example, and what does that memory suggest to you?

That said, not everything in a scrying is necessarily a fount of wisdom. One problem faced by beginners in scrying, especially those who don't have a lot of prior experience with meditation, is that stray thoughts and irrelevancies end up being woven into the scrying by the half-trained mind. Like a radio symbol in which the message is mixed with static, scryings by novice scryers often contain a mix of useful material and random imagery. As you meditate on each scrying, keep an eye out for things that seem clearly out of place.

Scrying can be a powerful tool for deepening your understanding of symbols and opening up the hidden potentials of human awareness, but it can also be an opportunity for many different kinds of foolishness, some of them relatively amusing, some a good deal less so. People have made spectacular blunders by blindly trusting information received from scrying and similar practices. The best way to avoid these pitfalls is to remember that scryings take place on the astral plane, the realm of dreams and imagination, and the information you receive in them may or may not have anything to do with the material plane where most of us live most of our lives. Common sense is just as important in occultism as it is in the rest of life!

Scrying and the Sacred Geometry Oracle

It may have occurred to you even before you read the example above that the cards of the Sacred Geometry Oracle could be used to create portal images for scrying. If so, you were quite correct. The deck was designed to be used for scrying as well as divination and meditation, and as you proceed with your explorations of sacred geometry and occult philosophy, one of the things you may wish to consider is to scry all 33 cards, meditating on the symbols you encounter in each session of scrying, as a way to deepen your understanding of the cards.

During the months you spend preparing for your initiation, however, something a little less demanding will be asked of you. What you need to do at this stage is three scryings: one of Card 4, The Circle; one of Card 7, the Equilateral Triangle; and one of Card 12, the Square.

You already know by now that these geometrical figures are among other things symbols of the Three Principles—the circle of Nwyfre, the equilateral triangle of Gwyar, and the square of Calas. You also know that the three figures when combined also form the Outer Emblem of the Order. In the course of your meditations on the cards of the Sacred Geometry Oracle, you will explore these figures further. Your task now is to go further by scrying with each of the figures and see what additional images and experiences you encounter while doing so. Scry each of the figures, note down what you experienced, and then meditate on the events, symbols, and information you encountered. All this will help prepare you for the ritual of initiation.

CHAPTER FIVE

Body practice

The ancient occult schools always included training for the body as well as for the mind. For complex historical reasons, however, the methods of body practice that were once used in the occult traditions of the Western world were lost many centuries ago, while the equivalent methods of the East remained in use. Over the last century occult schools in the West have borrowed and adapted a range of Eastern body practice systems to replace those that were lost. Members of the Golden Section Fellowship are encouraged to take part in this work by choosing such a system and making it part of their practice.

Some Eastern body practices in their original forms do not combine well with Western mystery school training, since they have been designed to support the specific forms of inner training practiced in their own cultural and spiritual settings. Fortunately the work of adapting many Eastern systems for Western bodies and Western occult training was taken in hand by capable teachers in the twentieth century, and the following systems have been found to work well with the practices of the Golden Section Fellowship.

Practicing one of the following body training methods is recommended but not required for members of the Golden Section Fellowship. If your health or circumstances don't permit you to take up one of these, simply continue with the rest of the work covered in this book. If you do have the opportunity to pursue one of these practices, though, you will find that the benefits that come from work of this kind are not limited to improved health, vitality, and fitness. The mental and spiritual skills developed by these forms of training will also improve your other practices and assist you in the quest for wisdom that is the heart of the Fellowship's work.

Aikido

Created in the mid-twentieth century by Japanese martial artist Morihei Uyeshiba, aikido combines self-defense training with ways of attuning with the One Life. Its name (pronounced "eye-key-dough") means "the way of unifying the life force." Aikidoka—practitioners of aikido—learn to blend their body's movements and energies with those of training partners, and also practice with traditional Japanese weapons such as sword and staff. To learn it you need to find a qualified teacher and invest several hours in practice two or three times a week at a dojo (training hall); fortunately these are easy to find in most Western countries nowadays.

Do-in

As mentioned in an earlier chapter, this ancient system of self-massage was brought from Japan and adopted by Druids in Brittany and France in the twentieth century. It uses rubbing, tapping, and stretching movements to balance the flow of the One Life in the body. Its name is pronounced "dough-inn," and means "guide and pull," because the exercises guide and pull life energy through the body's subtle channels It can be learned from books. Fifteen to thirty minutes a day is a good amount of time to invest in it; if your schedule permits, you can simply do this as an expansion of the closing self-massage at the end of your meditations.

Five Tibetan Rites

Introduced to the Western world in a book by occultist Peter Kelder in a 1939 book, and available these days on many websites and in many books, the Five Tibetan Rites are a set of simple, robust exercises that strengthen and balance the material and subtle bodies. They have been widely adopted by Western occultists since that time, and can easily be learned from books or videos. It takes between five and twenty minutes a day to practice the Rites.

Hatha yoga

The advanced forms of yoga practiced by sadhus and yogis in India can require years of training and close supervision by a qualified instructor. Fortunately many talented teachers have reworked hatha yoga to make it better suited to Western bodies and minds, and the forms of yoga now taught in schools all over the Western world are well suited to occult training. Yoga should be learned from a qualified teacher; the length of your daily practice session will depend on the specific style, school and tradition of yoga you choose to study.

Shintaido

Created in the 1960s by a group of Japanese martial artists under the leadership of Hiroyuki Aoki, shintaido is a movement art that can be applied to combat situations rather than a martial art in the narrow sense. Its name (pronounced "shin-tie-dough") means "new body way." Shintaido practice is based on a simple *kata* (pattern of movements) called Tenshingoso, from which other forms and movements unfold. It must be learned from a qualified instructor, and you should plan on practicing for several hours one to three times a week, depending on the schedule of classes at the dojo.

Tai Chi Chih

Created in the 1960s by American tai chi teacher Justin Stone, Tai Chi Chih is a set of nineteen movements and one posture designed to balance and strengthen the flow of the One Life through the body. It takes around twenty minutes a day to practice. The gentlest of the practices listed here, Tai Chi Chih is especially well suited to the elderly or those who have health impairments. It should be learned from an accredited instructor; once you've learned how to do it, however, you can practice it on your own for the rest of your life.

Other arts

The movement arts listed above are the ones that have been tested for compatibility with the work of the Golden Section Fellowship and have proved to be a good match for the Fellowship's system of occult training. There are doubtless many others that are just as compatible with the practices in this book. If you already have some form of body practice—be it a martial art, a healing art, a system of exercise, a sport, or something else entirely—by all means see how it works to continue that practice while taking up the work of the Fellowship.

Generally speaking, if a body practice doesn't include breathing exercises or ways of moving life energy through the body, you should have no problem combining it with the material in this book. The more a body practice relies on breathing exercises and work with life energy in the body, the more likely it is that these will conflict with the work of the Fellowship.

The sign to watch out for is some symptom of poor health that starts out small and becomes steadily worse over time. For example, you may find yourself becoming more and more tired, or more and more vulnerable to minor illnesses, or more and more easily chilled, or more and more easily overheated. If something like this happens, you should certainly consult a licensed health care provider to find out if something more ordinary is the matter, but in any case you should stop either your body practice or your occult work for at least three months. If the problem rights itself or your health improves noticeably, then there was an incompatibility between the practices and you will need to let go of one or the other.

One way or another, if you take up a body practice—and as mentioned before, this is optional rather than required—it may take some time and experimentation to find a practice that works for you and to figure out how much time to devote to it. Give yourself the time and the opportunities you need. As with the rest of the work of the Fellowship, your body practice is not a test to be passed, but a journey that will unfold over the years ahead.

CHAPTER SIX

Opening and closing a lodge

Now that you have learned how to do the Sphere of Protection and discursive meditation, and made the other practices and traditions of the Golden Section Fellowship part of your life, only one step remains before you can perform the initiation ritual and become a member of the Fellowship, a partaker in its life and energy and a companion on the road in the quest for wisdom. This final step is learning the opening and closing ceremonies for a lodge of the Fellowship. You will use these ceremonies to begin and end the initiation ritual, but they also play an important role in other parts of the Fellowship's work.

The opening and closing ceremonies are far from being mere formalities. They work with the energies of the Unseen, and they also embody certain core symbolic patterns used in the work of the Fellowship. Putting a week or two of daily meditations into the details of these ceremonies is a good way to start unpacking what they have to teach you.

If you followed the instructions given in Chapter Two for setting up your personal lodge and altar, everything you need for the opening and closing ceremonies is already in place. Once the chair is facing the altar and the altar has the three cauldrons, straightedge, and compass on it, you're ready to begin the opening.

Opening ceremony

The opening ceremony for a lodge of the Golden Section Fellowship is done as follows:

First, stand in your lodge in front of the chair, facing the altar, with incense burning in the central cauldron. Pause for a moment and clear your mind, then say aloud, "May the powers of Nature assist me to open this lodge of the Golden Section Fellowship in due form. Let peace first be proclaimed to the four quarters."

Second, face east and raise your right hand with the palm outward in salute. Say, "May there be peace in the east." Turn to face south, raise your hand in the same way, saying, "May there be peace in the south." Turn to face west and repeat the gesture, saying, "May there be peace in the west." Turn to the north, repeat the gesture, and say, "May there be peace in the north." As you do each of these, imagine peace and harmony flowing outward from your lodge to bless the four quarters of the world.

Third, face the altar again and say, "Since peace has been proclaimed, let this lodge be established, purified, and consecrated with the Three Principles."

Fourth, go to the altar, pick up the cauldron of salt, and raise it up as though in offering. Then bring it back down to somewhere around the level of your solar plexus.

You are now going to use the cauldron of salt to establish the boundaries of your lodge, by drawing a square around the lodge with it going clockwise, as shown in Diagram 6-1. Hold the cauldron in your left hand and go to your right, drawing a straight line from the altar to the corner of your lodge (which does not have to be the corner of the room). Make a right angle, and trace one side of the square; make another right angle, and trace another; make another and trace the third, and then a fourth right angle and another movement should bring you back to the altar and complete the square, as shown in the diagram. As you do this, imagine the cauldron drawing a line in emerald green light.

OPENING AND CLOSING A LODGE   89

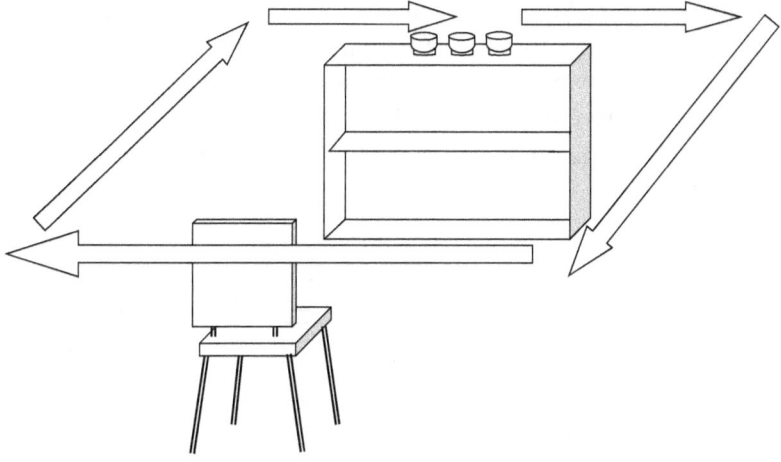

Diagram 6-1.

Fifth, put the cauldron of salt back in its place and pick up the cauldron of water. Raise it as though in offering, and then bring it back down to around solar plexus level. Now go around the lodge again, using the cauldron of water to draw a triangle surrounding the lodge, as shown in Diagram 6-2. As you do this, imagine the cauldron drawing a line in sky blue light.

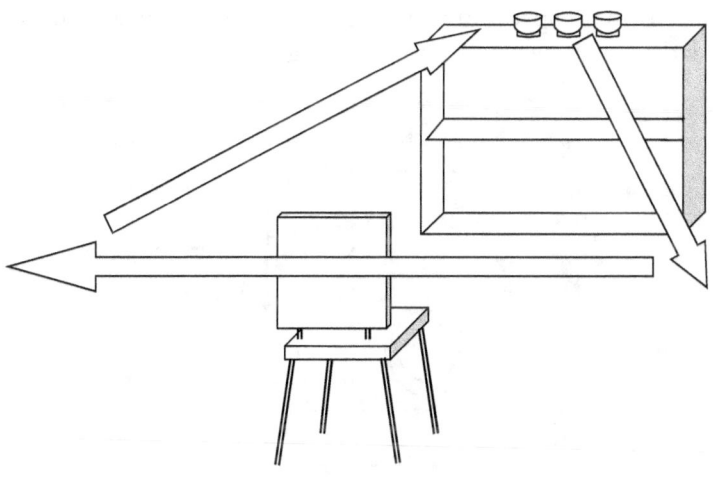

Diagram 6-2.

90   THE WAY OF THE GOLDEN SECTION

Sixth, put the cauldron of water back in its place and pick up the cauldron of incense. Raise it as though in offering and bring it back down to solar plexus level. Now go around the lodge a third time, using the cauldron to draw a circle surrounding the lodge, as shown in Diagram 6-3. As you do this, imagine the cauldron drawing a line in pure white light.

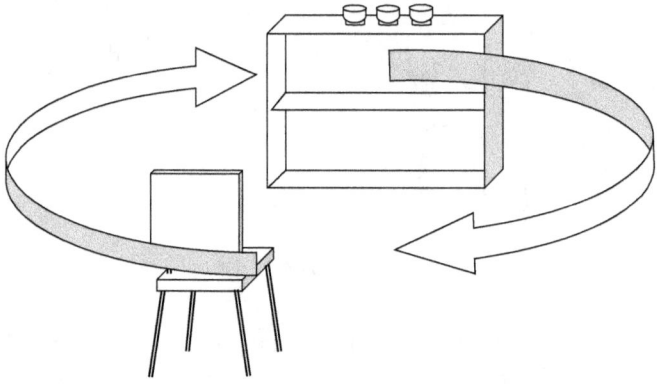

Diagram 6-3.

Put the cauldron of incense back in its place. The result of these movements, of course, is that you have drawn the Outer Emblem of the Fellowship in the space surrounding your chair and the working area of your lodge, as shown from above in Diagram 6-4.

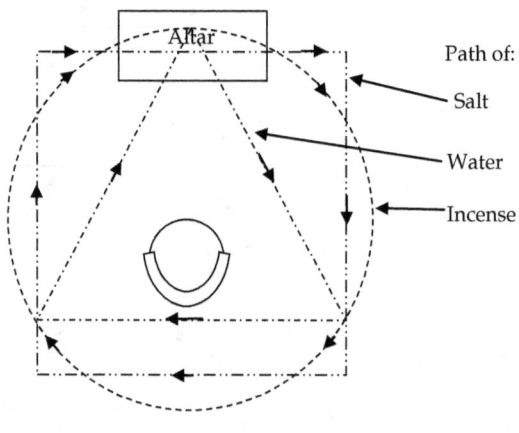

Diagram 6-4.

Seventh, stand in front of the chair again, and say aloud, "Let a Sphere of Protection now be formulated." Then perform the complete Sphere of Protection ritual. This is done in the same way you've learned already, but with one difference: you are placing the Sphere of Protection about your lodge rather than yourself. When you invoke the element of air, for example, you say: "By the yellow gate of the rushing winds and the hawk of May in the heights of morning, I invoke the Air and all its powers. May the powers of Air bless and protect this lodge this day and always, and further its work." Then, after thanking the powers of Air and tracing the symbol counterclockwise: "And with the help of the powers of Air, I banish from within and around this lodge all harmful influences and hostile magic and every imbalance of the nature of Air. I banish them far from this place." Change the words in the same way for each of the other six phases, and make sure the sphere of light at the closing phase extends out beyond the square, triangle, and circle you have traced around the lodge.

Eighth, when you have completed the Sphere of Protection, go to the altar. Put the straightedge in front of the central cauldron, open the compasses, and lay them atop the straightedge, in the form shown in Diagram 6-5 below, with the handle of the compass pointing away from you. This represents the Three Rays of Light that, according to the symbolism of the Druid Revival, brought the world into being.

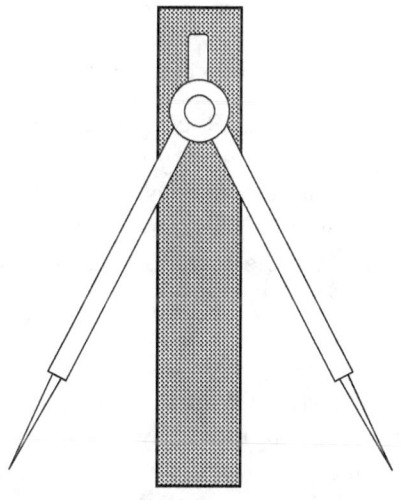

Diagram 6-5.

Ninth, step back and stand in front of the chair. Say the following: "With the help of the powers of Nature and in the name and the presence of the eternal Spiritual Sun, I declare this lodge of the Golden Section Fellowship open in due form." As you say this, imagine the sun high above the lodge, shining its rays down onto you. Hold this image for a while, and then sit down. This completes the opening ceremony, and you can now go on to the work of the lodge.

Between opening and closing

The opening ceremony you've just performed has created a sacred space in which many kinds of occult practice can be performed. The ritual of initiation is one of these, but only one. Once you are an initiated member of the Fellowship, you will find it helpful to open a lodge at least once a week and do some inner work in it before closing. For example, scryings are very often done in an open lodge, because the effects of the opening ceremony tend to make inner exercises yield better results. You can also simply make a habit of performing a sacred geometry exercise or reading a section of a sacred text or a book of wisdom in the open lodge. Whatever you choose to do within an open lodge, you will find that simply doing the opening and closing rituals help keep you connected to the inner dimension of the Fellowship—a dimension you will begin to experience in the ritual of initiation.

Closing ceremony

Whenever you have performed the opening ceremony, you should perform the closing ceremony before you return to ordinary activities. The closing ceremony is done as follows.

First, stand up, facing the altar. Pause for a moment and clear your mind, then say aloud, "May the powers of Nature assist me to close this lodge of the Golden Section Fellowship in due form. Let the quarters again be acknowledged."

Second, salute the east as you did in the opening, but this time say: "May peace abide in the east." Do the same thing in the south, west, and north, changing the words appropriately.

Third, face the altar again and say: "Since peace has again been proclaimed, let the lodge be unwoven and the Three Principles returned to their sources." You will now unwind and erase the pattern of subtle influences you created in the Opening Ceremony, using the cauldrons as before.

Fourth, go to the altar, pick up the cauldron of incense, and walk with it in a circle, going counterclockwise around the lodge. (This is the reverse of the movement shown in Diagram 6-3.) As you do this, imagine the cauldron absorbing and erasing the line of white light it drew in the opening. When you have finished and brought the cauldron back to the altar, raise it up as in salute, and then put it back in its place on the altar.

Fifth, pick up the cauldron of water, and proceed with it in a triangular pattern around the lodge, going counterclockwise. (This is the reverse of the movement shown in Diagram 6-2.) As you do this, imagine the cauldron absorbing and erasing the line of blue light it drew in the opening. When you have finished and brought the cauldron back to the altar, raise it up as in salute, and then put it back in its place on the altar.

Sixth, pick up the cauldron of salt, and proceed with it in a square pattern around the lodge, going counterclockwise. (This is the reverse of the movement shown in Diagram 6-1.) As you do this, imagine the cauldron absorbing and erasing the line of green light it drew in the opening. When you have finished and brought the cauldron back to the altar, raise it up as in salute, and then put it back in its place on the altar.

Seventh, step back from the altar to stand in front of the chair, facing the altar, and say: "Let any energies awakened in this working not needed to fulfill its purpose be returned to the Earth for her blessing." Imagine the subtle energies you have called into the lodge flowing down from the lodge to the heart of the Earth. Maintain the visualization for several minutes, or until the lodge room feels clear.

Eighth, imagine a golden sun high above the lodge, with rays streaming down. Say these words: "May all beings join in the contemplation. Let us contemplate the Light of Lights, the Sun of Suns, the unquenched flame within each living soul." Then, imagining every being in all the universe joining in these words: "May we receive enlightenment from that great Source."

Ninth, go to the altar. Close the compass and put it back in its place, and then put the straightedge back in its place. Then step back to stand in front of your chair and say: "With the help of the powers of Nature and in the name and the presence of the eternal Spiritual Sun, I declare this lodge of the Golden Section Fellowship closed in due form."

Understanding the opening and closing ceremonies

The opening and closing ceremonies have a great deal of complexity and richness underlying their apparent simplicity. Some of what they have to teach can only be learned by regular practice or by meditation on the symbols expressed or implied in the ceremonies, but a few comments may be helpful at this stage. Both rituals follow the same basic structure, and we can go through that structure a step at a time.

1. **The Announcement of the Work.** The subjective mind seems to work by something very like the famous rule pronounced by the Bellman in Lewis Carroll's *The Hunting of the Snark*: "What I tell you three times is true." Accordingly, it's very common to begin an occult ceremony by saying what you are going to do, then to do it, and finally to say what you have done. The first of these, the announcement of the work, also helps cue your subjective mind to turn its attention to the business at hand. It is a prologue to the ceremony.
2. **The Proclamation of Peace.** This comes from Druid tradition. By saluting the four quarters and proclaiming peace to them, you are symbolically placing your lodge and its work at the center of a balanced and harmonious cosmos. This part of the ceremony also represents the One Life.
3. **The Weaving and Unweaving of the Principles.** Since your lodge can be in a space you use for other purposes as well, you need a way to establish sacred space temporarily, and then to return the space to its ordinary condition. This part of the ceremony is where that happens. By tracing the square, the triangle, and the circle around the space you establish the symbolic boundaries of your lodge and strengthen them by the Three Principles. This part of the ceremony also, of course, represents the Three Principles.
4. **The Sphere of Protection.** This serves the same function in the lodge ritual that it does in your daily practices; it brings you into balance with the powers of the Unseen and places you in contact with the elements of creation. In the closing ceremony, the sending of the energies to the Earth and the contemplation of the Eternal Spiritual Sun reconnect you to Spirit Below and Spirit Above respectively. This part of the ceremony also represents the Seven Gates.
5. **The Placement of Compasses and Straightedge.** This comes from the old craft guilds, of which Freemasonry is one of the few

survivors. In the ceremonies of the guilds, placing two of the working tools of the craft in a special position on the altar signaled that the meeting was open for whatever business came before it, and when the working tools were moved out of that position, the meeting was closed. That tradition was picked up by occult schools long ago, and it appears in various forms in the ceremonies of those schools.

6. **The Declaration.** This has the same function as the Announcement of the Work, as discussed earlier.

If you've been paying attention, you may be wondering by now why the opening and closing ceremonies have six parts rather than seven. In fact, they each have a seventh part! The seventh part of the opening ceremony is the work that is done within the open lodge. The seventh part of the closing ceremony is returning to your ordinary activities.

CHAPTER SEVEN

The ritual of initiation

The work presented in this book all leads to your ritual of initiation, which will mark the beginning of your journey with the Golden Section Fellowship. As you have learned already, the word "initiation" literally means "beginning," and the ritual of initiation is meant to begin a new phase in your life and of your participation in the quest for wisdom discussed in Chapter One.

You may be wondering, with that in mind, why the ritual of initiation was not given to you on the first page of this book! The reason, of course, is that the Golden Section Fellowship is a path of self-initiation. No one else can perform the ritual of initiation for you, and that means that you have to prepare yourself by a series of basic practices, both so that you have the skills to perform the ritual effectively, and so that you are in an appropriate state to receive the benefits of the ritual.

Most traditions of occultism and spirituality expect the novice to spend some time in preliminary studies before they are considered ready to begin the work of the tradition. For that matter, the old craft guilds that inherited some of the lore of sacred geometry required beginners to become apprentices and gain some basic skill in the craft before going further. Treat this period of preparation in the same spirit, and it will become part of the process by which you begin your journey in search of ancient wisdom.

Before your initiation

In order to perform the ritual of initiation you need to have learned all the practices covered in this book. As already noted, no one else can do the ritual for you, and so you have to have achieved a basic level of competence with the work before your initiation, so you can do it effectively. For the ritual, you need to be able to do the following things from memory:

- The Sphere of Protection;
- Discursive meditation;
- Scrying;
- Divination using *The Sacred Geometry Oracle*;
- The lodge opening and closing ceremonies.

During your period of preparation, you should plan on doing the following things:

- Become familiar with the symbols discussed in Chapter One.
- Make the morning and evening exercises and the solar plexus exercise from Chapter Two part of your daily routine, and experiment with affirmations and journaling to the extent that feels appropriate to you.
- Practice daily divination with *The Sacred Geometry Oracle*, using the method set out in Chapter Two.
- Practice the Sphere of Protection ceremony daily, so that you can do the complete version of that ceremony, as explained in Chapter Three.
- Complete all the preliminary stages of learning to meditate, and devote at least one session of meditation to each of the cards of *The Sacred Geometry Oracle*, as discussed in Chapter Four.
- Do all of the geometrical exercises given in the book that accompanies the *Oracle*.
- Perform the three scryings described in Chapter Four.
- Consider whether you will be taking up a body practice as part of your work in the Golden Section Fellowship, as discussed in Chapter Five, and if you choose to do so, start to learn that practice.

Finally, you need to learn how to construct the Outer Emblem of the Golden Section Fellowship in the traditional way, using a straightedge and compass only. Instructions for this are given below.

All this will take you at least two months of preparation, and quite possibly more than this. Take your time and be thorough, remembering that this period of preparation is essential to the initiation. Without the preparation, the initiation ritual is an empty formality. With the preparation to establish the subtle patterns that give life to any ceremony, the initiation ritual becomes an empowerment, a turning point in your inner life and the beginning of a quest for wisdom that can last for the rest of your life.

Constructing the Outer Emblem

Since sacred geometry is one of the core practices of the Fellowship, you should plan on picking up some skill with the geometer's tools—compass and straightedge—before your initiation. The geometrical exercises included in *The Sacred Geometry Oracle* are excellent practice for this, and as already noted, you should do all of them at least once before your initiation. Before you perform the ceremony of initiation, you should be able to follow the instructions for drawing a geometrical diagram accurately. To test your skill, you must be able to construct the Outer Emblem of the Fellowship—the familiar circle, triangle, and square pattern, with each of these in the correct proportion to the others—using nothing but compass, straightedge, and pen.

The instructions for drawing the Outer Emblem are as follows:

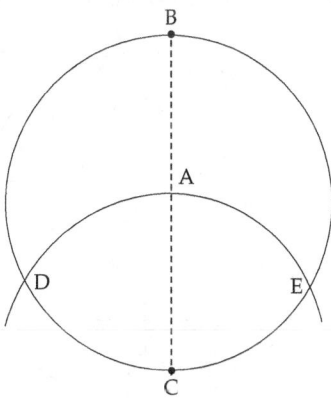

Diagram 7-1.

Using the compass, draw a circle; its center is point A. Then, using the straightedge, draw a line through the circle, passing through point A; this line is marked BC in the diagram.

Once you have done this, with the compass still set to the same distance between the points you used to draw the circle, put the center point of the compass on point C and draw an arc cutting across the circle at points D and E.

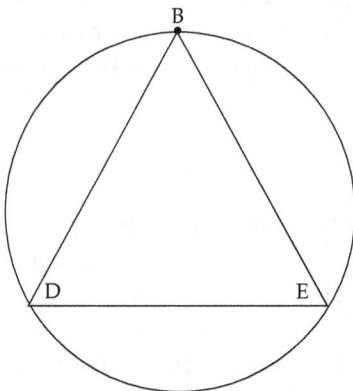

Diagram 7-2.

Using the straightedge, draw a line from B to E, from E to D, and from D to B, creating the triangle within the circle. If you have done this right, the three sides of the triangle will be of identical length. (Check this by setting the compasses so that they reach from D to B, and then see if they reach exactly from E to B and from E to D.)

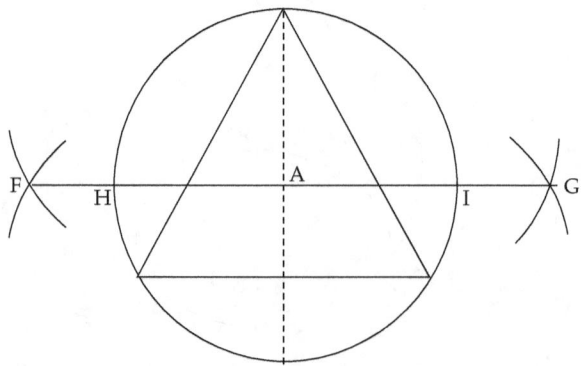

Diagram 7-3.

THE RITUAL OF INITIATION   101

Now set the compass wide. Put the center end on point B, and draw a little arc off to each side as shown. Put the center end on point C without changing the compass setting, and do the same thing, so that the two little arcs cross at points F and G. Draw a line from F to G, crossing the circle at points H and I. This line should go through point A at the circle's center and divide line BC exactly in half. (Again, check this with your compass.)

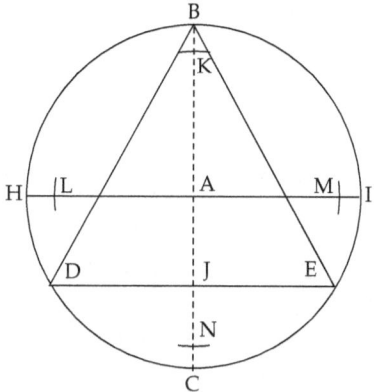

Diagram 7-4.

Put the center end of the compass on point J, where line BC crosses line DE, and set the width between the compass points to the distance between J and D (or J and E—these two distances should be identical). Now, without changing the compass setting, put the center end on the central point of the circle, and draw little arcs cutting lines BC and HI at K, L, M, and N.

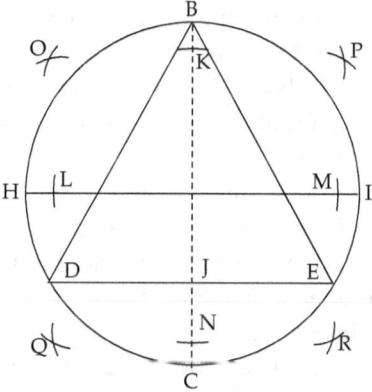

Diagram 7-5.

Now, leaving the setting of the compass points unchanged, place the center point of the compass on points K, L, M, and N in turn, drawing two little arcs to each side, and thus marking the points O, P, Q, and R.

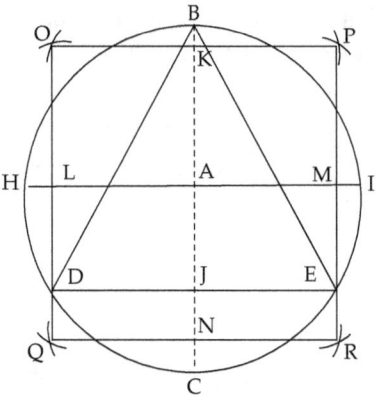

Diagram 7-6.

Finally, using the straightedge, draw lines from O to P, P to R, R to Q, and Q back to O. Line OP should go through point K, line PR through points M and E, line RQ through point N, and line QO through points D and L. This completes the construction; the original circle, triangle BDE, and square OPRQ form the Outer Emblem of the Fellowship, with the circle, the triangle, and the square all in their correct proportions.

By doing this, you have also accomplished one basic form of one of the classic constructions of sacred geometry: the squaring of the circle. It's impossible, using compass and straightedge alone, to construct a square and a circle of exactly the same circumference, or of exactly the same area—but it's possible to come very close. The construction of the Outer Emblem manages both of these tasks to within a respectable margin, the sort of margin that was common in the construction of stone circles and ancient temples.

It's worth taking a moment to work out the numbers. It's standard practice to set one of the measurements in a sacred geometry construction equal to 1, and so we'll do this with the radius of the original circle. The circumference of a circle equals twice the radius multiplied by π, *pi*, the irrational number that begins 3.1415927... and continues out to infinity. The area of a circle equals the radius squared and then multiplied by π. So the circumference of our circle is $(1 + 1) \times \pi = 6.2831854...$ and so on, while the area of our circle is $(1 \times 1) \times \pi = 3.1415927...$

The sides of the square are the same length as the sides of the triangle, and an equilateral triangle inscribed in a circle has sides equal to the radius of the circle multiplied by $\sqrt{3}$, the square root of 3, which equals 1.7320508... and so on out to infinity. Since the radius of the circle equals 1, the sides of the square equal $\sqrt{3}$. The circumference of a square is the length of one side multiplied by 4, and the area is the length of one side squared. The circumference of our square is therefore 4 x 1.7320508... = 6.9282032..., and the area is $\sqrt{3}^2$, which is of course 3.

6.9282032... isn't 6.2631854...—the difference is a little over 9% of the larger number—and 3 isn't 3.1415727...—the difference here is a little under 5%. It's possible to get a much closer fit between circumferences or between areas, using compass and straightedge, though the closer you get to one, the further you get from the other! For a relatively simple construction, however, the Outer Emblem does a respectable job of squaring the circle: close enough to guide the builders of stone circles and temples in ancient times, and certainly close enough to guide the first efforts of a new initiate.

Once you have worked your way through the geometrical exercises in the book that accompanies *The Sacred Geometry Oracle*, you should have no trouble working through the construction of the Outer Emblem. You will need to have the construction drawn out on a sheet of paper before you perform the initiation ritual. Yes, you can make several attempts if you need to! Check your work with the compasses in the ways described in the instructions above, and make sure the proportions are right. Once you have drawn the Outer Emblem and completed all the other steps listed earlier, you are ready to be initiated into the Golden Section Fellowship.

The initiation of the golden section fellowship

To perform this ritual, you will need an hour or so free from interruption. You will also need your lodge with the furnishings described earlier, and the Outer Emblem of the Fellowship, drawn on paper in the way described above.

Set up your lodge for the opening ceremony, with fresh water in the cauldron of water and a stick of incense (or fresh pot pourri) in the cauldron of incense. Have your chair ready in its usual place. Put your copy of the Sacred Geometry Oracle deck and a pen and paper or a notebook near your chair, so you can cast a reading and write down the results.

Then leave the room, taking the Outer Emblem with you, close the door and sit down in another chair. Look at your drawing of the Outer Emblem, and think about the three geometrical figures that form it: the circle, the triangle, and the square. Each of those figures is rich with symbolic meaning. Think about what the book that comes with *The Sacred Geometry Oracle* has to say about these three figures, and about the results of your three scryings.

When you are ready, go to the door of your lodge, bringing the diagram with you, and tap gently on it seven times, as though seeking admission. Then open the door, go into your lodge room, and close the door behind you. At this point the ritual proper begins.

First, stand in front of the chair, facing the altar, and after you have taken a moment to clear your mind, say the following words out loud: "Comes now [say your full name here], who has completed the preparatory studies in the ancient wisdom and now seeks initiation into the Golden Section Fellowship."

Second, step forward and set your drawing of the Outer Emblem on the altar, and say aloud, "I present this work of my hands as evidence that I have completed the preparatory studies in due form." Place your right hand palm down on the Outer Emblem. "And on this Outer Emblem of the Fellowship, I pledge that if I am accepted as an initiate of the Fellowship I will pursue the study and practice of the ancient wisdom, in whatever form it may present itself to me, and I pledge likewise that if I am accepted I will be a true and honorable companion to all those who share that commitment, to the extent that they behave as true and honorable companions toward me."

Third, step back to stand in front of the chair, facing the altar. Then perform the complete opening ceremony as you have been taught to do it.

Fourth, when you have proclaimed the lodge open in due form, sit in the chair facing the altar. Settle your body into the posture of meditation, relax, and do five minutes or so of the Fourfold Breath, as you would do to prepare for meditation or scrying. What you will be doing here is something a little different from either of these exercises, though it resembles scrying in some ways. Its proper name in occult writings is the Composition of Place.

Fifth, as you sit there in your chair facing the altar, imagine that the room around you dissolves outward, and you find yourself sitting in the midst of the forest. Great trees rise around you, soaring high above you and letting stray beams of sunlight slant down to the forest floor. You are sitting on a block of roughly carved white stone, and the altar before you is a larger block of the same white stone; on the altar are three small cauldrons holding salt, water, and incense, and a compass and straightedge made of bronze, placed together as in an open lodge. Propped against the side of the altar to your right is a wooden staff. Draped across the side of the altar to your left is a length of rope divided by knots, with a loop at one end.

Take your time building up this image, and bring in all your imagined senses: feel the cool age-smoothed stone beneath you, hear the rustling of wind in the leaves high above, smell the forest-scents of soil and bark and leaf and, mixed in with them, the tang of incense from the altar. Make it as vivid as you can before proceeding.

Sixth, see a wise teacher come out from between the trees and approach the far side of the altar. The teacher is bareheaded and barefoot, with long white hair, and wears a robe of plain unbleached cloth tied by a cord belt with many knots in it; the other details, including the teacher's gender, are left up to your imagination. Again, take the time to imagine the teacher as vividly as possible.

Seventh, when you are ready, the teacher says to you, "I welcome you to the Lodge in the Forest, where all initiates of the Golden Section Fellowship have come to receive their initiation. Before you may receive the same gift, I must ask you certain questions. Why do you seek initiation into our Fellowship?"

Answer this out loud, in your own words.

"Have you pledged yourself, upon the Outer Emblem of the Fellowship, to pursue the study and practice of the ancient wisdom, and to be a true and honorable companion to all those who share that commitment, and behave as true and honorable companions toward you?"

Answer this out loud, in your own words.

"Will you keep that pledge, to the best of your ability?"

Answer this out loud, in your own words.

"It is well," says the teacher. "Rise, and approach the altar."

Eighth, rise to your feet and go to stand before the altar, continuing to imagine yourself in the midst of the forest, standing before an altar of white stone and facing a wise teacher.

"Take this staff," says the teacher, and hands it to you; you imagine yourself taking it in your right hand. "In olden times, when seekers after wisdom traveled to far places, staffs such as this helped them make their way safely over rough roads and defend themselves from attack. Yet the staff has another meaning, for this is the earliest form of the straightedge, and our ancient brothers and sisters used wooden staffs like this to trace straight lines upon the earth.

"Take this measuring cord," says the teacher, and hands it to you; you imagine yourself taking it in your left hand. "In olden times, when seekers after wisdom gathered in hidden assemblies in forests and deserts, knotted cords such as this worn as rope belts served as a badge of fellowship that identified them to one another. Yet the measuring cord has another meaning, for this is the earliest form of the compass, and our ancient brothers and sisters used cords such as these along with wooden stakes to trace out circles and arcs upon the earth.

"Down through the ages, our customs and ceremonies have changed with the changing times. Your straightedge shall therefore be your staff, and your compass your measuring cord. Place the staff upon the straightedge."

You imagine doing so. As you lower the staff, however, it shrinks in your hand, and becomes the straightedge upon your altar.

"Place the measuring cord upon the compasses." You imagine doing so, and the measuring cord shrinks in your hand and becomes the compass upon your altar.

Ninth, the teacher says, "Now take a pinch of salt between the thumb and first finger of your left hand." You do this—not only in imagination, but taking an actual pinch of salt from your bowl or cauldron. "Say aloud, 'With this salt I establish myself as an initiate of the Golden Section Fellowship.'" You repeat the words aloud. "Now touch the salt to the point between your eyebrows, then to your solar plexus, then place it in your right palm, rub your palms together, and draw them suddenly apart, scattering the salt." You do these things as instructed.

Tenth, the teacher says, "Next, dip the fingers of your right hand into the water." Again, you do this with the material water, not only in imagination. "Say aloud, 'With this water I purify myself as an initiate of the Golden Section Fellowship.'" You repeat the words aloud. "Flick a few droplets onto the upper part of your face, then do the same to your solar plexus, and then rub your hands together." You do these things as instructed.

Eleventh, the teacher says, "Next, pick up the cauldron of incense in your left hand." Again, you do this with the material incense, not only in imagination. "Say aloud, 'With this incense I consecrate myself as an initiate of the Golden Section Fellowship.'" You repeat the words aloud. "Now, with your right hand, wave the scent of the incense toward the point between your eyebrows, then toward your solar plexus. Then set the cauldron of incense back down, and hold your right hand palm down over it, then your left hand, so that the smoke of the incense touches both palms." You do these things as instructed.

Twelfth, when you have finished, the teacher raises both hands and extends them above your head, and says, "With the help of the powers of nature, and in the name and the presence of the Eternal Spiritual Sun, I declare that you, [your full name], have been initiated into the Golden Section Fellowship in due form." The teacher lowers both hands. "Be seated, and meditate on what you have beheld. Know that from this hour onward, the subtle influences of the Fellowship will help guide you as you pursue your quest for the ancient wisdom. I leave you now in peace." The teacher bows slightly to you in farewell, and leaves the altar, vanishing from sight among the tall trees of the forest.

Thirteenth, sit down in your chair, facing the altar, and meditate on the entire inner dimension of the ritual: the Lodge in the Forest, the wise teacher, the questions you were asked, the staff and measuring cord, and the blessings of salt and water and incense. Call all these things back to mind, and understand as much of them as you can at this stage. Don't be troubled if there are things about the ritual you do not understand; those will become clear later on.

Fourteenth, cast a Sacred Geometry Oracle reading of three cards. The first represents you, the second represents your situation in the world, and the third represents the work that lies before you as an initiate of the Golden Section Fellowship. If any of the cards are reversed, read them as challenges you will need to face and overcome as you proceed. Note down the reading and your interpretation of it.

Fifteenth, perform the complete closing ceremony as you have been taught to do it. This completes your ritual of initiation. You are now an initiate of the Golden Section Fellowship.

After your initiation

Once you become an initiate, the real adventure begins. How you choose to pursue that adventure is up to you. The most important thing is to keep learning, studying, and practicing. There are many different fields of occult knowledge you may choose to take up—so many that you may have a hard time choosing among them! Two subjects are particularly recommended for you to consider, however.

The first of these is sacred geometry. As you already know, this is central to the teaching and work of the Fellowship. Until a few years ago, there was very little available in print on the subject, and several of the most popular books on the subject muddled up geometrical ideas with odd theories about aliens and conspiracies. Fortunately things have improved since then, and the books listed in the Resource section of this book will give you plenty of options to start with.

The second of these subjects is astrology. The sort of thing you see in newspaper astrology columns is not real astrology. Real astrology, when it explores the personality and destiny of the individual, works not with the birth sign alone but with the complete birth chart, showing the positions of the sun, moon, and planets as seen from the place and time of birth. There are also other branches of astrology that have nothing to do with birth charts, such as mundane astrology (the astrology of politics and nations), electional astrology (the art of timing events to take advantage of astrological forces), horary astrology (the art of answering questions using astrology), and much more. There are many good books on astrology, and more are being published every year, so it's easier than ever before to gain a good working knowledge of the science of the stars.. If you choose to take up this branch of occult study, you will never run out of things to learn.

Basic practices and meditation

The basic practices you learned first—the morning exercise, the evening exercise, the solar plexus exercise, affirmations, and journaling—should remain a regular part of your life as you proceed with the work before you; the first of them, as explained shortly, will take a slightly different form now that you are an initiate. Discursive meditation should also remain one of the foundations of your spiritual life. Once you begin studying some branch of occult knowledge, whether that be sacred geometry, astrology, or something else, you can use what you learn in your studies as a source of themes for meditation, and you can use the symbols you encounter in your studies as a source of portal images for scrying. You'll find that discursive meditation and scrying will enable you to get far more out of your studies than you can get by any other means.

The body practice you took up during your time of preparation, if you chose to do so at that time, is another thing worth making a regular part of your life as you follow the quest for wisdom, revelatoin, and enlightemnent. If you didn't take up a body practice, you can always do so at any point you feel drawn to do so. Furthermore, if you find that the practice you chose doesn't suit you, or simply want to explore the range of possibilities, you can always try something else. Many students of occultism experiment with several different body practices before finding one that meets their needs for the long term.

The initiate's morning exercise

As noted above, the version of the morning exercise practiced by initiates of the Golden Section Fellowship is a little different from the version you have been practicing up to this point. The difference is small but important. As you breathe in and breathe out during the practice, imagine that the breath is not simply moving through your nostrils—feel it flowing in through every pore in your skin all over your body, and feel it flowing out the same way. Imagine the breath, as it flows in, bringing the One Life with it, vitalizing and renewing every cell of your body. As it flows out, imagine it carrying away tensions and impurities with it.

The art of pore breathing, as it is sometimes called, is taught in many occult schools, and it is well worth learning and practicing. Over time, as you work with it morning after morning, it will stop being something you have to imagine and become something you can feel. As you become used to it, you will find that your ability to work with the One Life in ritual and in everyday life will gradually increase.

The initiate's sphere of protection

As an initiate, you can also expand the Sphere of Protection in certain ways. The actions and most of the imagery you will use remains unaltered; the opening and closing also remain the same. Certain changes, though, are made to the words you will use for the callings of the seven gates. Here is how it's done; you may of course continue to invoke Deity in the practice if you choose, in the way discussed in Chapter Three. (The new words added to the ritual are in *italics*.)

First, perform the Opening exactly as you have already been taught.

Second, invoke Air in the east in the usual way, saying these words: "By the yellow gate of the rushing winds and the hawk of May in the heights of morning, I invoke the Air and all its powers. May the powers of Air bless and protect me this day and always, and further my work. *May they help me attain helpful attitudes and true insights.*" When you have contemplated Air for a time, say, "I thank the powers of Air for their gifts." Then banish with Air in the usual way, saying these words: "And with the help of the powers of air, I banish from within me and around me and from all my doings all harmful influences and hostile magic, *all negative habits of mind*, and every imbalance of the nature of air. I banish these far from me."

Third, invoke Fire in the south in the usual way, saying these words: "By the red gate of the bright flames and the white stag of the summer greenwood, I invoke the Fire and all its powers. May the powers of Fire bless and protect me this day and always, and further my work. *May they help me attain appropriate desires and firm decisions.*" When you have contemplated Fire for a time, say, "I thank the powers of Fire for their gifts." Then banish with Fire in the usual way, saying these words: "And with the help of the powers of Fire, I banish from within me and around me and from all my doings all harmful influences and hostile magic, *all negative habits of will*, and every imbalance of the nature of Fire. I banish these far from me."

Fourth, invoke Water in the west in the usual way, saying these words: "By the blue gate of the mighty waters and the salmon of wisdom in the sacred pool, I invoke the Water and all its powers. May the powers of Water bless and protect me this day and always, and further my work. *May they help me attain helpful relationships and balanced emotions.*" When you have contemplated Water for a time, say, "I thank the powers of Water for their gifts." Then banish with Water in the usual way, saying these words: "And with the help of the powers of Water, I banish from within me and around me and from all my doings all harmful influences and hostile magic, *all negative habits of emotion*, and every imbalance of the nature of Water. I banish these far from me."

Fifth, invoke Earth in the north in the usual way, saying these words: "By the green gate of the tall stones and the great bear of the starry heavens, I invoke the Earth and all its powers. May the powers of Earth bless and protect me this day and always, and further my work. *May they help me attain robust health and provide for my material needs.*" When you have contemplated Earth for a time, say, "I thank the powers of

Earth for their gifts." Then banish with Earth in the usual way, saying these words: "And with the help of the powers of Earth, I banish from within me and around me and from all my doings all harmful influences and hostile magic, *all negative habits of body*, and every imbalance of the nature of Earth. I banish these far from me."

Sixth, invoke Spirit Below in the usual way, saying these words: "By the orange gate of spirit below and the power of the telluric current, I invoke Spirit Below and all its powers. May the powers of Spirit Below bless and protect me this day and always, and further my work. *May the telluric current arise and fill me with life.*"

At this point you add one of the new visualizations. Breathe in a slow deep breath, and as you do so, imagine the telluric current bubbling up through the soles of your feet like cool, sparkling spring water. Imagine it flowing up into your entire body, filling it with a feeling of vitality. As you breathe out, feel the current remaining in your body, and say, "I thank the powers of Spirit Below for their gifts."

Seventh, invoke Spirit Above in the usual way, saying: "By the purple gate of spirit above and the power of the solar current, I invoke Spirit Above and all its powers. May the powers of Spirit Above bless and protect me this day and always, and further my work. *May the solar current descend and fill me with light.*"

At this point you add the second of the new visualizations. Breathe in a slow deep breath, and as you do so, imagine the solar current streaming down through the top of your head like clear bright sunlight. Imagine it flowing down into your entire body, filling it with a feeling of lightness and brightness. As you breathe out, feel the current remaining in your body, and say, "I thank the powers of Spirit Above for their gifts."

Eighth, invoke Spirit Within in the usual way, saying: "By the six powers here invoked and here present and the secret of the lunar current, and in the Grand Word AWEN, I invoke Spirit Within. May the powers of Spirit Within me bless and protect me this day and always, and further my work. *May the lunar current be born in me and kindle the Inner Flame.*"

At this point you add the third and most important of the new visualizations. As you breathe in, imagine the energies of the solar and telluric currents inside you drawing together into your solar plexus and becoming a golden sphere of light, like a little sun a few inches across. As you breathe out, imagine a slender line of light rising up from the solar plexus along the midline of your body to the center of your head, where it kindles a little flame like the flame of a candle, but the pure white color of starlight. Repeat this two more times, drawing the energies together into an inner sun on the inbreath and sending a line of light up to the center of your head on the outbreath. (It's important to send the line of light up the midline of your body and not up your spinal cord; I'll explain why shortly.)

Ninth, say: "By that flame, and with the help of all the powers I have invoked, I establish about myself a Sphere of Protection." Then perform the closing visualization in the same way as before. This completes the initiate's Sphere of Protection.

Understanding the initiate's sphere of protection

Two important differences set the initiate's Sphere of Protection apart from the version you learned earlier in this book. The first of these differences is that, having learned to work with the energies of the seven elements, you can begin to direct those energies more specifically to things that you need to bring about in yourself and your life. The words of the first four callings given above will give you some idea of how this can be done. Plan on using those four callings exactly as given for one year, so you can get a good sense of what you can expect from this approach. After that, you can change them if you wish, using the rules for affirmations to come up with appropriate words.*

The three visualizations in the last three callings are of course the other important difference, and they have a different end in view. To understand this, it helps to know a little more about the human nervous system. You learned earlier that each of us has two minds, an objective mind centered in the brain and a subjective mind centered in the solar plexus. They are joined by the spinal cord, which begins in the brain and reaches the solar plexus via branching nerves, but they also have another link: the vagus nerve, which descends from the underside of the brain and connects to the solar plexus and the nerves that control your vital organs.

---

*My book *The Druid Magic Handbook* goes into much more detail about ways to use the Sphere of Protection for practical purposes; the version of the Sphere used in that book is somewhat different, but all the methods taught there can be used with the ritual as given in this book.

One of the secrets of occultism is that nerves can do more than carry messages to and from your brain. They also serve as channels for the One Life. Many people these days have heard of kundalini yoga—a way to enlightenment that guides a current of the One Life up the spinal cord from the tailbone up to the brain, awakening a series of centers along the spine that connect to the body's glands. This is a powerful method but a dangerous one, and it has to be done under the supervision of an experienced teacher to avoid the risk of serious illness.

A subtler and safer way of doing the same thing works by way of the vagus nerve rather than the spinal cord. This is what you are doing with the three added visualizations in the initiate's Sphere of Protection. You draw energies from the Unseen into your body, concentrate them in your solar plexus, and send them up the vagus nerve to the brain. If this makes you think of the fusion of solar and telluric currents into the lunar current, good—you're paying attention. That is exactly what's going on here. In a relatively safe and gentle way, you're creating the lunar current inside yourself.

That creation takes place in the pineal gland: a small gland in the center of your head, underneath the two halves of your brain. The pineal gland has the same basic structure as an eye, but it is not sensitive to ordinary light; in occult texts it is sometimes called the Eye of Revelation. It is the organ through which we can attain wisdom, revelation, and enlightenment. As you stimulate it gently with the One Life, you will notice an increase in mental clarity, and you will begin to develop the sixth and seventh senses—the sense that perceives the One Life, and the sense that perceives consciousness itself.

Working in your lodge

At least once each week, you should also use the lodge opening ceremony to open a lodge of the Golden Section Fellowship, and then close the lodge again with the closing ceremony once you've finished. (Use the ordinary Sphere of Protection ritual, without the additional words and visualizations, in the opening ceremony.) As mentioned back in Chapter Six, many people find that scryings are more effective when done in an open lodge. You can also simply make it a habit to open a lodge and then spend a little while reviewing what you've learned over the past week, and deciding where you want your studies to go next.

Working in an open lodge has certain benefits for you as an initiate. As you learned from the Introduction, the Golden Section Fellowship exists primarily in the Unseen, and the lodge ritual is the most important way for you to make contact with it there. With regular practice of the lodge ritual, you will establish a connection through which guidance and help will come to you. The guidance and help will likely be very subtle at first—a helpful coincidence here, a sudden hunch there—but as you learn to notice it, it will become easier to notice and follow.

There is another side to the work you do in your lodge, however. The traditions from which the Golden Section Fellowship derive its teachings and heritage place a high value on independent, individual work, but they also make room for groups of initiates working together in lodges. One of the long-term goals of the Fellowship is the establishment of lodges of this second kind. The rituals these will perform are much more elaborate than those you have learned in this book, but they follow the same underlying patterns. As you open and close your home lodge, therefore, you are learning skills that may someday make it possible for you to open and close a lodge with other initiates of the Fellowship, and you are also establishing patterns in the Unseen that will help bring such lodges into existence.

As I mentioned in the introduction, this book is part of an experiment. There's no way to know in advance what results that experiment will have. It might simply succeed in reviving a certain amount of interest in classic occult teachings, and teaching a certain number of readers how to make occult study and practice part of their lives. It might succeed in helping to bring about a network of occult lodges where the individual quest for wisdom, revelation, and enlightenment can become the basis for group workings. It might go beyond that, and succeed in rediscovering certain ancient secrets that have been lost for centuries. As an initiate of the Golden Section Fellowship, you are contributing to the success of that experiment as you pursue your own search for the ancient wisdom. Welcome to the quest!

APPENDIX ONE

Exercises for the 33 Emblems

Each of the thirty-three cards of *The Sacred Geometry Oracle* has a geometrical exercise associated with it. As noted earlier, you will need to do each of these exercises at least once before you perform your ritual of self-initiation; they are presented in the book that comes with the Oracle, but are included here also for convenience.

Exercise for Emblem 1

For this exercise, you'll need the usual tools of the sacred geometer mentioned in the Introduction—pen, straightedge, and compass—but you won't actually use any of them! Simply set them down in front of you, along with a piece of blank, unlined paper. Look at the paper, and think about the various patterns you could draw on it with the tools you have. Imagine points, lines, arcs, circles, triangles, squares, and more complex designs as well. Picture them on the paper ... and then let the images fade, and return your attention to the plain blank surface of the paper in front of you. Do this for a few minutes at least, and do something else before you go on to any of the other exercises in this book.

The point of this exercise may be clear to you as soon as you do it, or it may not. This actually doesn't matter that much. It's useful to remember that in sacred geometry, as in so much of life, it's more important to do things than to understand them intellectually. If you have a strongly visual imagination and pay attention to the instructions, it's possible to do any of the exercises in this book in your head, but most of the lessons they have to teach will remain hidden from you unless you actually pick up the tools of sacred geometry and do the exercises right here in the material world.

Exercise for Emblem 2

As you did with the exercise for Emblem 1, take the three tools of sacred geometry—the pen, the straightedge and the compass—and set them down in front of you, along with a sheet of plain, unlined paper. In this exercise, you'll be using only the first of the tools, the pen. The point and the pen are linked symbolically as well as practically; in both these two senses, the business end of the pen is nothing but a point, a way of marking position in the unbounded, undefined space of the blank tracing board.

Start out by considering the sheet of paper in front of you, as you did in the exercise for Emblem 1, imagining the different patterns you can bring into being on its blank surface. Then. slowly, deliberately, and with intent, make a mark somewhere on the paper: a single dot, as small as you can make it.

Now consider the paper again. Whatever you do with the paper from this time on, that point will play a role. Even if you deliberately draw a pattern that doesn't relate to it at all, it will be there, suggesting connections and relationships by its simple presence. Go ahead and imagine different patterns on the paper, as before, but see how the point you have drawn interacts with them and shapes them.

When you've done this for a few minutes, set the paper aside. Don't throw it out; you'll need it for the next exercise.

Exercise for Emblem 3

For this exercise, you'll need your pen and straightedge, and the sheet of paper marked with a single point from the exercise for Emblem 2.

Set the paper before you, consider it, and then mark a second point on the paper, wherever you like. (The only requirement is that it shouldn't be precisely on top of the first point!)

Once you've drawn the second point, take your straightedge and line it up on the two points. If at all possible, the straightedge should extend off the edge of the paper on both sides. With your pen, draw the line that connects the two points, and extend it out to the edge of the paper in both directions. Set the straightedge aside, and consider the line for a few moments; try to see how it unites and separates at the same time.

If you like, repeat this exercise several different times, marking your two points in different places on the paper and extending the lines accordingly. Practice positioning the straightedge so that the line you draw with it goes exactly through the two points; if you don't have much experience with practical geometry or drafting, this will help a good deal with some of the more detailed geometrical exercises to come.

Exercise for Emblem 4

For this exercise, you'll need your pen and compass, and several sheets of unlined paper. As in the exercise for Emblem 3, mark one point on the paper, then another; the two should be close enough together that the two points of your compass can reach easily from one to the other.

Decide which of the two points will be the center of your circle, and put the metal point of the compass exactly onto it, pressing the point into the paper. Widen or narrow the compass until the pencil point comes exactly to the other point, and then twist the handle around to draw a circle, starting and ending at the other point.

If you haven't used a geometer's compass before, it may take you a certain amount of practice before you can do so with any degree of grace. Take the time you need; you'll be drawing a lot of circles in the exercises to come.

A couple of technical terms will help make things clearer in later exercises; if you managed to miss geometry in school, or have forgotten whatever you learned then, you may want to make mental notes. The curved line that you draw with the pencil point of the compass, marking the outer edge of the circle, is called the circumference. A straight line that goes through the center of the circle, dividing the circle in half, is called a diameter. Half a diameter—that is, a line going from the center to the circumference in one direction—is called a radius. An arc, finally, is simply part of a circle: a curved line, drawn with a compass, that doesn't go all the way around to connect up with itself.

Exercise for Emblem 5

For this exercise, you'll need some items that aren't normally part of the modern geometer's toolkit. A pushpin (the sort with a cylindrical plastic head), a piece of string around eight inches long, and some tape will be needed, along with a pencil and a sheet of unlined paper. You also need to find a table or working surface in which you can stick a pin solidly without causing damage you or anyone else will regret later. (If you don't want to mar your desk or table, try putting a piece of tagboard or heavy poster board underneath the paper.)

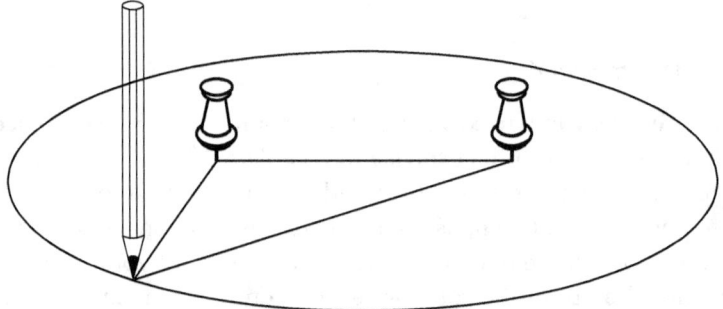

Drawing the ellipse.

    Start by tying the two ends of the string together with a knot that won't slip—a square knot works well—to form a loop. Next, stick the two pushpins into the paper, a few inches apart, and make sure they're fixed firmly in the working surface. Loop the string around the pushpins, and put the pen or pencil in the loop and pull it out until the string is taut, forming a triangle, before putting the point down against the paper.
    At this point, all you need to do is move the pen or pencil to one side, keeping the string loop taut at all times. Let the string slide freely around the pen or pencil and the pushpins. The movement of the pen

or pencil and the pull of the string loop will combine to trace a perfect ellipse on the paper, with the two pushpins as its two foci.

Exercise for Emblem 6

For this exercise you'll need your pen and compass, along with a sheet of paper. Start by marking two points on the paper, just as in the exercise for Emblem 3; choose one as the center, set the points of the compass to equal the distance between them, and draw a circle around the center point, beginning and ending at the other. For convenience, we'll call the two points A and B, with A at the center of the circle you've just drawn.

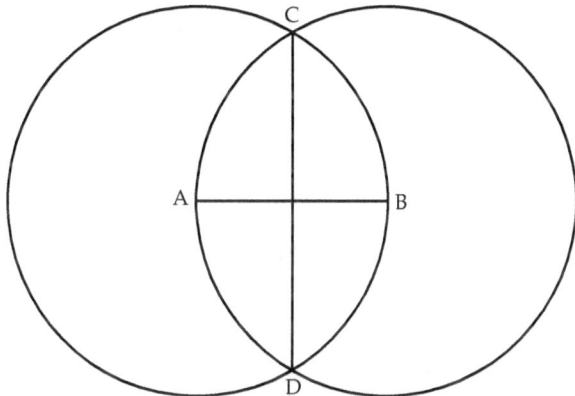

Drawing the vesica piscis.

Then, without changing the distance between the compass points, put the metal point of the compass on point B, where the pencil point started, and the pencil point where the metal point was, on point A. Draw another circle, this time with point B at the center, overlapping the first circle to form a vesica piscis.

The two points where the circles cross are important, so mark them as points C and D. If you were to measure the distance between points A and B, and compare it to the distance between C and D, you would find that if your vesica is drawn correctly—no matter how large or small it happens to be—the relationship between the two distances is always the same: the longer distance (the length of the major axis, in geometer's jargon) is always equal to the shorter distance (the length of the minor axis) times $\sqrt{3}$, the square root of 3.

Exercise for Emblem 7

Start by drawing a line somewhere not too far from the middle of the paper. On the line, mark two points, which should be labeled A and B. They can be as close or as far apart as you like, but whatever distance you choose will be length of the sides of your triangle, so plan accordingly.

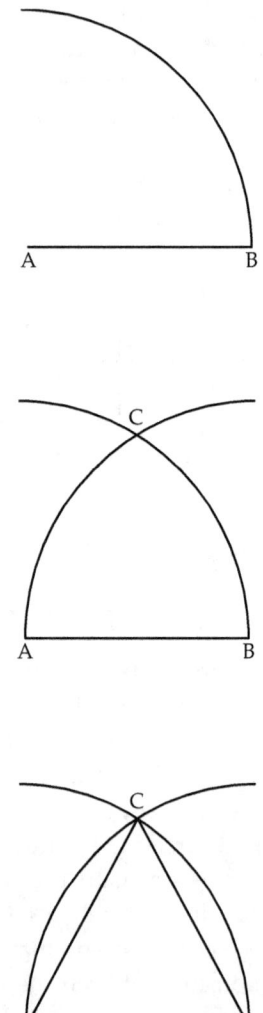

Drawing the equilateral triangle.

EXERCISES FOR THE 33 EMBLEMS   121

(For example, don't put them so far apart that the third point of the resulting triangle will end up off the paper!)

Put the metal point of the compass on point A, and adjust the pencil point until it rests on point B. Draw an arc up from B until you've made at least a quarter-circle. Now, without changing the setting of the compass points, put the metal point on B, set the pencil point on A, and draw an arc up from A until it crosses the first arc. Mark the point where the arcs cross as point C. (If you've been paying attention, you've probably realized already that this whole process is simply a matter of drawing half a vesica piscis; if you extend the arcs as far below line AB as you did above it, the whole vesica will be formed.)

Then, using the straightedge, draw a line to connect A and C, and another one connecting B and C, to create triangle ABC, just as shown in the diagram.

Exercise for Emblem 8

Start the exercise for this emblem by using your compass to draw a circle of any convenient size, and mark a point, point A, on the circumference of the circle. With the setting of the compass points unchanged from drawing the circle, put the metal point of the compass on A, and draw an arc as shown in the diagram, crossing the circle's circumference on both sides. If you're paying attention, you'll notice that the arc goes through the mark left by the compass point at the center of the circle, and this may give you a clue about the deep patterns underlying this construction.

Mark points B and F where the arc crosses the circumference, as shown. Then move the metal point of the compass to B and draw another arc, crossing the circumference at A and a new point, which should be marked as point C. Do the same with the metal point at F, crossing the circumference at A and a new point E.

Now do the same thing twice more, once with the metal point at C and once with it at E. If you've placed your points where they should be—and this is a good test of how carefully you're handling the compass—the arcs from C and E should meet at a new point, D, which is exactly opposite your original point A. (If they don't meet, try to figure out where the mistake is, and either correct the drawing you have or give it another try.)

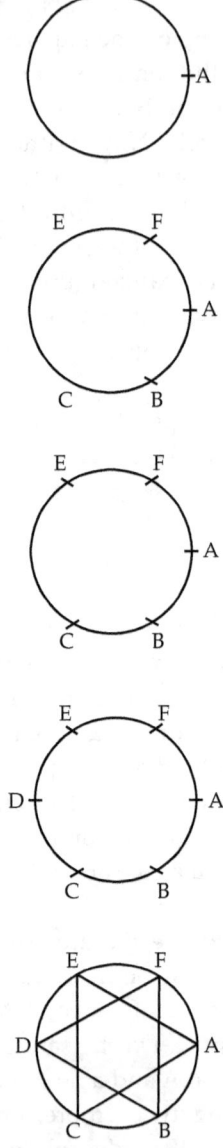

Drawing the hexagram.

Finally, using the straightedge, draw lines connecting points A and C, C and E, E and A, B and D, D and F, and F and B, to create your hexagram.

EXERCISES FOR THE 33 EMBLEMS   123

Exercise for Emblem 9

The exercise for this emblem is based on the vesica piscis, but it moves in new directions, and introduces a method we'll be using in many

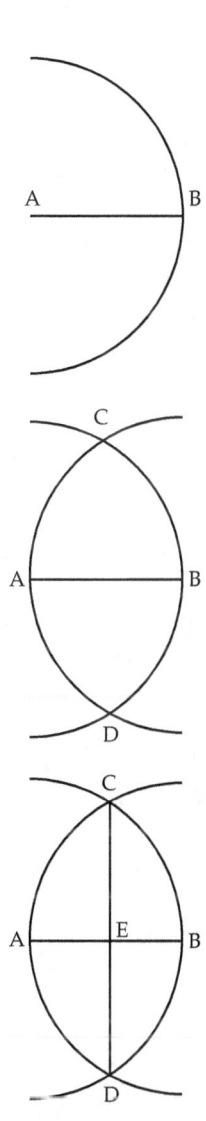

Drawing the cross.

of the exercises to come. You may wish to pay careful attention to the following steps, and practice the method several times to make sure you've worked out any difficult parts.

Start by drawing a line, and marking points A and B on it. Now make a vesica with line AB as the minor axis: that is, set the compass points to the distance between A and B; with A as the center point, draw an arc up and down from B, through a half-circle; then, with B as center, draw an arc up and down from A, crossing the first arc above and below the line. Mark the points where the two arcs cross as C and D. Using the straightedge, draw in line CD, and where it crosses line AB, mark point E.

The two lines AB and CD now form a right-angled cross, with point E as its center. It's worth mentioning that, if you followed the instructions, E will be exactly halfway between A and B, and also exactly halfway between C and D. Any time you need to divide a line segment in half geometrically, this is a quick and effective way to do it.

Exercise for Emblem 10

In geometrical terms, a right triangle can be constructed in a number of ways. The exercise that follows does the trick using the vesica and the cross.

Start by making a vesica and unfolding a cross from it, just as in the last exercise; if you like, you can simply use the same sheet of paper. Next, choose any two points you like, one somewhere on line BC, the other somewhere on line DE. (To make the process of drawing clearer, neither point should be too close to A, although geometrically speaking any point beside A itself is fair game.) Label these points F and G.

With the straightedge, draw in line FG. No matter where you put F and G, triangle AFG will be a right triangle, because all four of the angles made by the crossing of the lines at E are right angles. You may wish to draw in a number of different points and lines, and consider the resulting triangles.

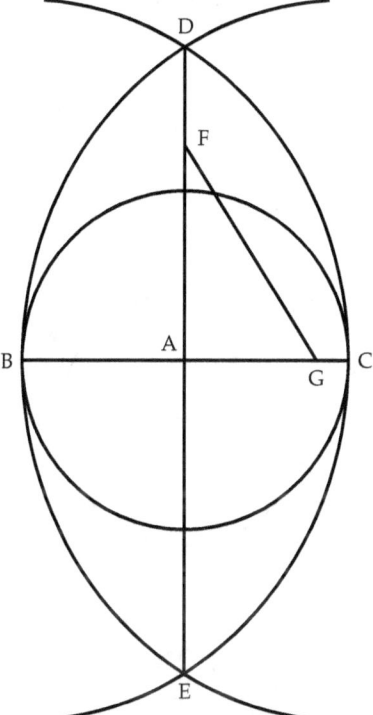

Drawing the right triangle.

Exercise for Emblem 11

This exercise, like the last one, uses the construction of the cross from the vesica that was introduced in the exercise for Emblem 9. Begin by marking point A somewhere near the center of the paper, and drawing a circle around it, using the compass. (The circle should be no more than half as wide as the sheet of paper, or you'll run off the edge of the paper later on in this construction.)

Then, with the straightedge, draw a line that goes through point A at the center of the circle and extends out to the circumference on both sides. Where the line cuts across the circle's edges, mark points B and C. Now, using line BC as the starting point, construct a vesica piscis outside the circle: set the compass points to the distance between B and C, and first with B as center, then as C, swing a pair of arcs up and down to intersect above and below the circle, forming the vesica.

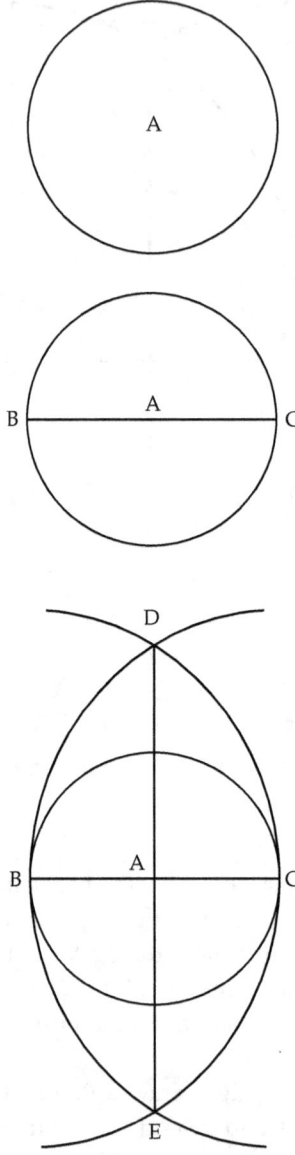

Drawing the quadrature of the circle.

Mark points D and E at the two ends of the vesica's major axis, and draw line DE. If you've followed the instructions, it should pass through point A, the center of the circle, and form a right-angled cross with line BC, accomplishing the quadrature of the original circle.

Exercise for Emblem 12

There are several different ways to construct a square geometrically, but the one we'll use here unfolds from the patterns we've already used.

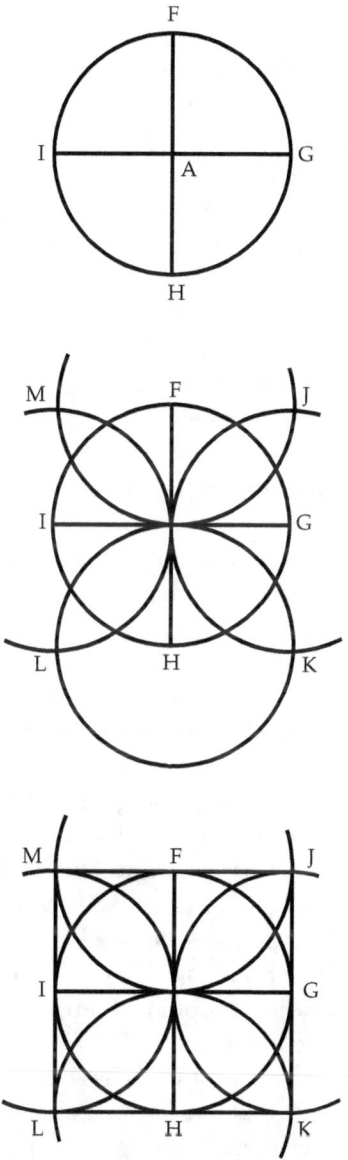

Drawing the square.

128   THE WAY OF THE GOLDEN SECTION

Start by following the instructions for the exercise for Emblem 9, exactly as given; if you prefer, you can simply take the design you made in that exercise, and use it for this one. It's possible to make a perfect square simply by connecting the four points where the lines of the right-angled cross intersect the circle, but there's another way to unfold a square from the quadrated circle that's a little more interesting.

First, mark the four points where the cross intersects the circumference of the circle; label them points F, G, H, and I. Then, set the compass points so that they are exactly the same distance apart that they were when you drew the original circle. (This is critically important.) Check your measurement by putting the metal point of the compass on point A, and making sure that the pencil point comes exactly over the circumference of the circle.

Once the compasses are set correctly, put the metal point on point F and swing an arc around through at least half a circle, making a vesica piscis with the original circle and leaving plenty of arc on either end, as shown. Do the same thing with points G, H, and I as centers, producing a flowerlike pattern. The ends of each arc should cross two others; mark points J, K, L and M at the crossings. Then draw in lines JK, KL, LM, and MJ to create square JKLM, which (again, if you've followed the instructions exactly) should fit precisely around the original circle.

Exercise for Emblem 13

For this exercise, besides plain paper and your geometer's tools, you'll need a pair of colored pencils or pens, of two different colors. Start by drawing a circle of any convenient size with your ordinary pen (or pencil). Draw a line across the circle, passing through its center; mark points A and B where the ends of the line cross the circle's circumference. Next, draw two arcs with A and B as centers and the compass points set to the distance between A and B; the result will be a vesica piscis surrounding your original circle. Line up the straightedge on the two points of the vesica, and draw in a line from one side of the circle to the other, going through the circle's center; mark points C and D where this second line intersects the circle's circumference.

Then, put the metal point of the compass on C, set the compass to the distance between C and A, and draw a circle all the way around. With the compass setting unchanged, move the metal point to A and make a pair of small arcs—just long enough to cut across the second circle in the two

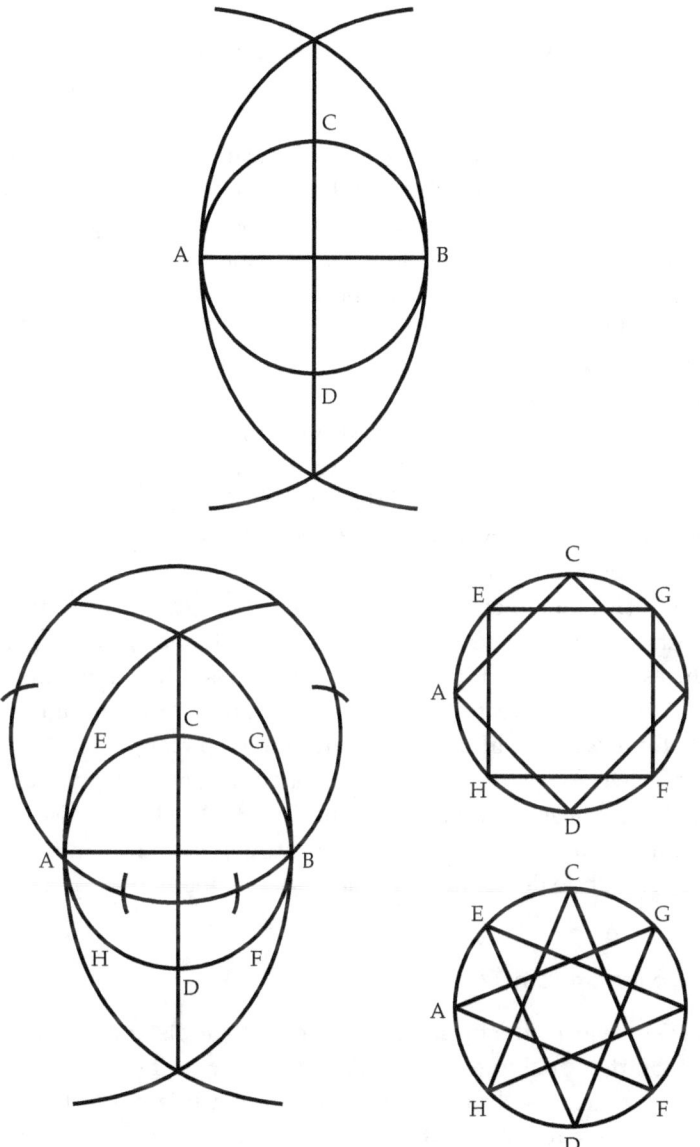

Drawing the octagram.

places where the compass reaches it, one outside the first circle, the other inside. Then do the same thing with the metal point of the circle on B, drawing two more short arcs and cutting the second circle in two places.

Now line up the straightedge on the places where the two short arcs you made with A at the center cross the second circle. (If you've done this correctly, the center of the first circle will fall exactly on the line.) Using this, draw a line running from one edge of the first circle to the other; mark points E and F where the first circle and the line intersect. Do the same thing with the places that the two short arcs made with B as center cross the second circle—again, the straightedge should just touch the first circle's center—and draw another line across the first circle from edge to edge, marking points G and H where the line crosses the circumference.

If you've done all this successfully—and the division of a circle into eight equal parts is no mean work for a beginner—you may not be happy to find out that all this is just preparation for the actual exercise! Still, the exercise itself is simple once the framework is in place. With one of your colored pencils and the straightedge, draw lines connecting points AC, CB, BD, DA, EG, GF, FH, and HE, as shown. This forms the same type of octagram shown on the emblem.

Then, with the other colored pencil and the straightedge, draw lines connecting points AG, GD, DE, EB, BH, HC, CF, and FA, as shown. This produces a different kind of octagram, which is called a unicursal octagram ("unicursal" means "following one route," since you can draw the whole thing without lifting your pen from the paper.)

These two forms of the octagram have different traditional meanings, and they also have a different intuitive feel, yet both arise from the same pattern of points equally spaced around a circle. This is a reflection of the subtle flexibilities built into sacred geometry.

Exercise for Emblem 14

This exercise uses the basic set of geometer's tools and plain, unlined paper. Start by using your compass to draw a circle of any convenient size. Then, with a straightedge, draw a line going through the center of the circle and extending out to the circumference on both sides. Mark points A and B at the two places where the line crosses the circumference.

Next, starting at point A, follow the instructions in the exercise for Emblem 6 to construct a hexagram; your compass should stay set to the width you used to create the original circle.

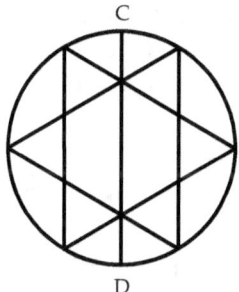

Drawing the dodecagram.

Now choose a point where the lines making up the two triangles cross. (Any of the six points of intersection will do equally well.) Line up the straightedge on the point you've chosen, and the center of the circle; you'll find that it goes through another point of intersection on the opposite side of the center. Draw a line through the point and the circle's center, extending it all the way to the circle's circumference on both sides. Mark points C and D where the line crosses the circumference of the circle. Now, just as before, follow the instructions given in the exercise for Emblem 6, and construct a second hexagram. The two hexagrams join together to create a dodecagram.

If you want to explore all the possible forms of the dodecagram, repeat the exercise, drawing in the lines of the triangles very lightly, and mark the points where the triangles intersect the circumference of the circle. The form of the dodecagram you've already drawn connects every fourth point around the circle—count the points as you go around from the point of one triangle to the next point of the same triangle, and you'll see how this works. If you connect every third point, you'll get a dodecagram made of three squares, instead of four triangles; if you connect every other point, you'll get a dodecagram made of two hexagons, while if you connect every fifth point, you'll get a unicursal dodecagram. Each of these has its own symbolic meaning and its own place in sacred geometry.

Exercise for Emblem 15

For this exercise, besides the usual tools, you'll need a pair of sharp scissors or a craft knife, and some clear tape; you can also use a heavier type of paper than usual. Start as in the exercise for Emblem 11, by drawing a circle, and then another circle of the same size, with its center on the first circle's circumference. Choose one of the two points where the

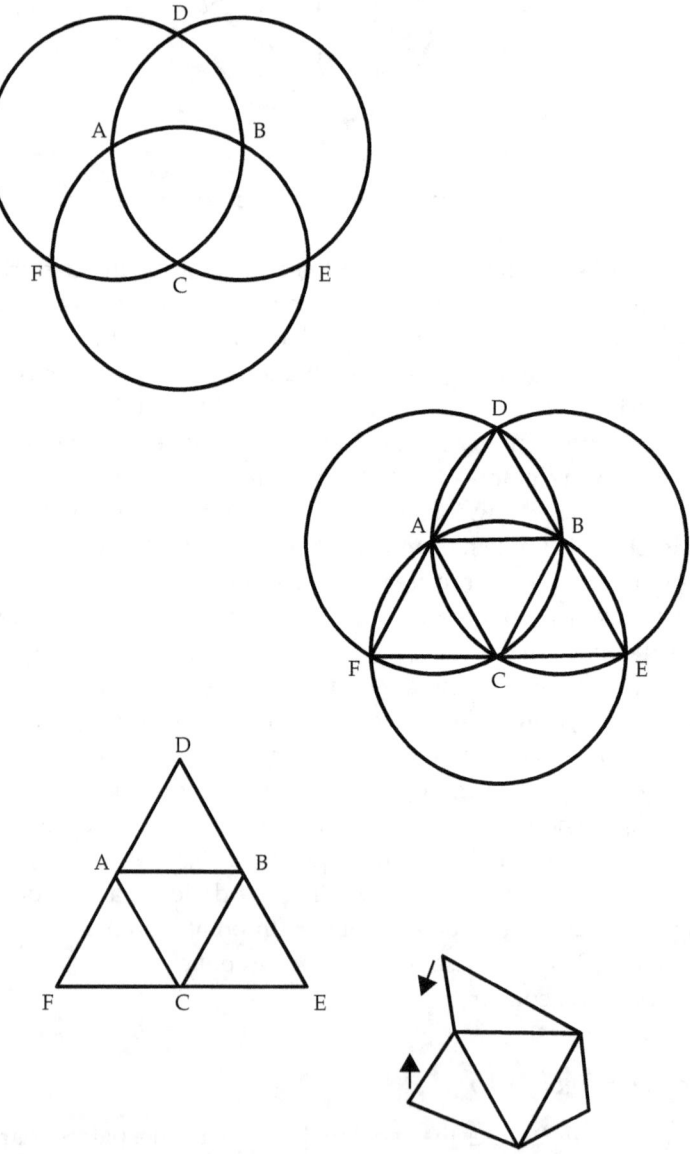

Constructing the tetrahedron.

circumferences of the two circles cross, and make a third circle of the same size with its center on that point.

You now have a pattern of three overlapping circles, forming three overlapping vesicas. In the center of the pattern is a space like a rounded triangle, where all three circles (and all three vesicas) overlap. Mark points A, B and C at the corners of this space. Then mark points D, E and F at the outward corners of the three vesicas. The result should look like the diagram.

Using the straightedge, draw in lines AB, BC and CA to form triangle ABC, and draw in lines DE, EF and FD to form triangle DEF. Triangle ABC is in the center of DEF, and the parts of DEF that are outside ABC form three more triangles, each of them identical to ABC.

Now, with the scissors or knife, cut along lines DE, EF and FD to separate triangle DEF from the rest of the paper. Carefully fold the paper along AB, BC and CA, creasing the paper along these lines, so that the three points D, E and F come together, forming a tetrahedron. Use pieces of tape to join the edges and make your tetrahedron stable.

Once you've made your tetrahedron, examine it from all sides, see how it fits together, and try to make sense of it on an intuitive level. If you like, mark points in the center of the four sides, and try to see how these become the points of another, smaller tetrahedron in the middle of the one you've made.

Exercise for Emblem 16

As with the exercise for Emblem 16, this one will call for scissors or a knife, and a roll of tape, along with your usual geometer's tools. Heavy paper may also be worth using.

This construction starts out like the last one, with a pair of circles drawn to form a vesica piscis, and a third circle drawn with its center on one of the two points where the first two circles intersect. To this you need to add three more circles, as follows. The fourth has its center where the third circle intersects with one of the first two; the fifth, where the fourth intersects with the same one of the first two; and the sixth, where the fourth and the fifth intersect. (Actually, of course, each circle intersects with its neighboring circle at two different places, but if you do the construction as given, you'll find that one of these intersections is always the center of another circle already.) The result is the zigzag pattern of six circles shown in the diagram.

Constructing the octahedron.

Now draw in the pattern of eight triangles shown in the diagram, using the straightedge. Cut the resulting shape out, cutting only along the outside lines—don't cut between any of the triangles you've drawn! Fold the resulting shape along the lines so that the two lines marked AB are joined together, and fold down the remaining triangles. Use tape to fasten the seams, and you have your octahedron.

As before, take the time to get to know the octahedron, looking at it from different angles and seeking an intuitive sense of the way it fits together. If you like, mark a point in the center of each of its eight sides, and try to see how these become the corners of a small cube in the center of the octahedron.

Exercise for Emblem 17

Like the last two constructions, this one requires tape and scissors or a knife, along with your geometer's tools, and may benefit from heavy paper as well. This exercise is one of the trickier constructions in this book; you'll want to be as careful as possible when drawing the lines and circles, so that the result comes out.

Start exactly as in the last exercise, by drawing two overlapping circles, then a third centered on one of their intersections, then a fourth, fifth and sixth, forming a zigzag pattern of circles, all of them overlapping and forming a double line of vesicas. This time, though, keep on going. You need no less than twelve circles, arranged as in the diagram, to construct an icosahedron. When you've drawn them all out, use the points of intersection to lay out the pattern shown in the diagram.

As before, cut out the pattern, cutting only the outside edge—again, don't cut between any of the triangles, or the result will be a mess! Fold the resulting shape so that all the points marked A come together, and all the points marked B are joined. Fasten the edges with tape, and you have your icosahedron. Take the time to explore it, and if you like, mark a point in the center of each of the twenty sides, and try your hand at imagining how these points become the corners of a small dodecahedron in the middle of the icosahedron.

136 THE WAY OF THE GOLDEN SECTION

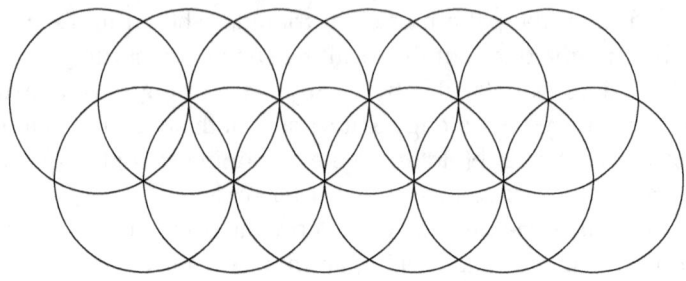

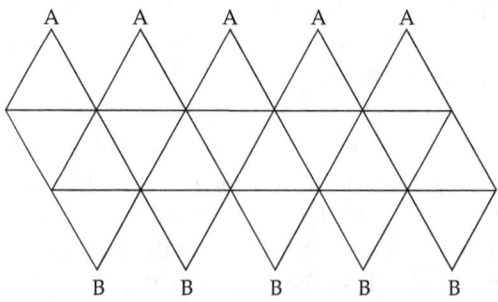

Constructing the icosahedron.

Exercise for Emblem 18

As with the exercises for Emblems 15, 16 and 17, this one works a little better with stiff paper, and a sharp craft knife or a pair of scissors is also

EXERCISES FOR THE 33 EMBLEMS   137

needed, along with your geometer's tools. Start by drawing a square of any convenient size, using the construction from the exercise for Emblem 12.

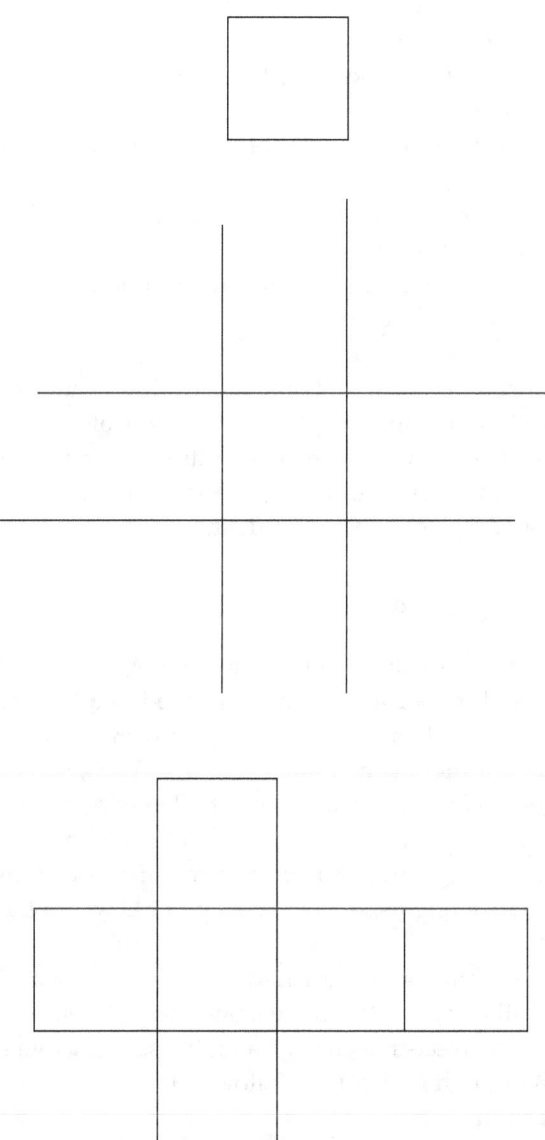

Constructing the cube.

Next, line up your straightedge with each of the four sides of the square, one at a time, and extend the lines out in both directions. Then set the compass points to the length of one side of the square, and with the metal point set at each of the four corners in turn, draw short arcs to mark off the same distance out from each corner along the lines you've drawn. Connect the marks together as shown, to make four more squares around the first.

This gives you five of the sides of your cube. To make the sixth, you simply need to repeat the same process one more time, putting the metal point of the compass on the two outer corners of one of the four new squares and making two new marks further out along two of the lines extending from the original square. Connect these marks to each other to form the sixth square.

Then cut around the outside edge of the pattern—again, don't cut between the squares. Fold and tape the resulting pattern to create your cube. Turn it around and about, looking at it from different sides and seeing the different patterns created by its sides and edges; if you like, mark points in the center of its sides, and try to imagine the octagram formed by linking these points inside the cube.

Exercise for Emblem 19

For this exercise, the usual set of geometer's tools and a plain sheet or two of blank paper are all that's needed. Start by constructing a square, as follows. Draw a line of any convenient length, and mark the two ends of the line as points A and B. Then, somewhere off the line (but not too far away!) and closer to B than A, mark point C. With the metal point of your compass on C and the width set to the distance between C and B, draw a circle; its circumference should cross line AB somewhere along its length. Mark point D where the line and the circle cross.

With the straightedge, draw a new line from D through C, and extend it further until it crosses the circle again above B. Mark point E where the new line intersects the circle. Using the straightedge again, draw a line from B through E. If you've followed the instructions, the angle at B is a right angle.

From this point making the square is simple. Put the metal point of the compass on point B, set the width to the distance between A and B, and swing an arc up one-quarter of a circle until it crosses line BE. Mark point F at the intersection. Leaving the compass at the same setting, put the metal point on F and draw an arc up from B at least a quarter circle, then move the metal point to A and do the

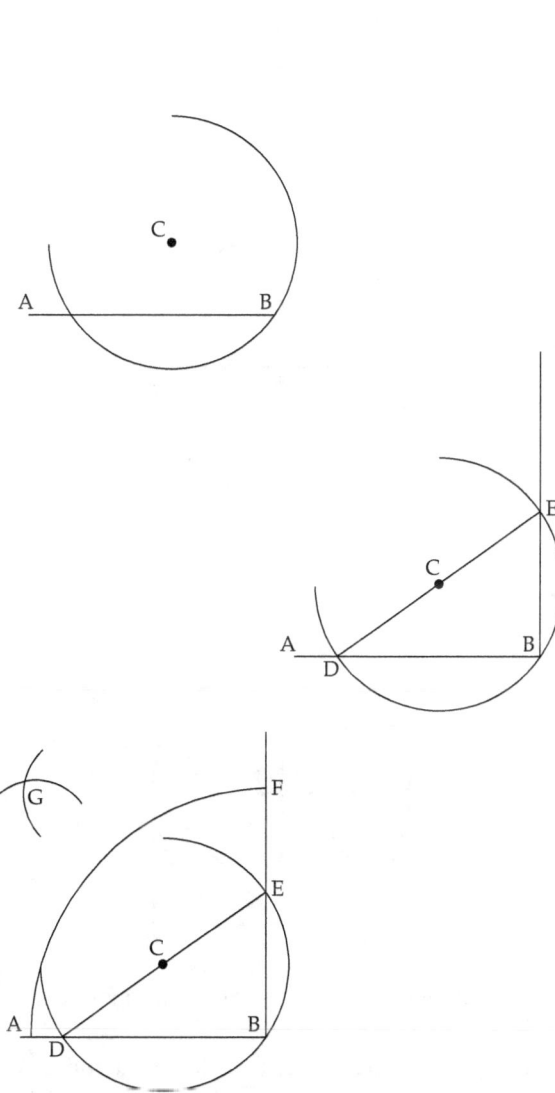

Drawing the square and diagonal.

140   THE WAY OF THE GOLDEN SECTION

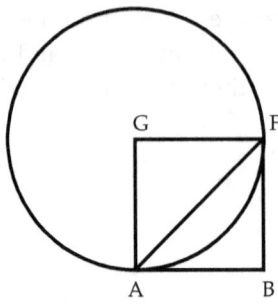

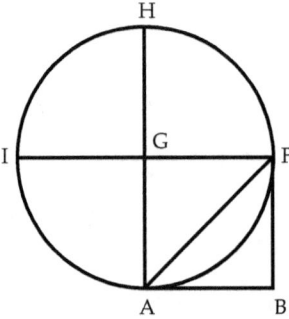

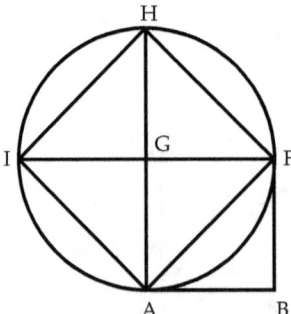

Drawing the square and diagonal.

same thing, so that the two arcs cross to form the fourth corner of the square. Mark this as point G. Draw in lines FG and AG to complete the square ABFG.

Draw in line AF, the diagonal of the square. Then put the center point of the compass on G, and with the compass still set to the distance from A to B, draw a circle. (The circumference should pass through A and F.) Using the straightedge, extend line AG to the far edge of the new circle; where the line meets the circumference, mark point H. Then do the same thing with line FG; where the extended line meets the circumference of the new circle, mark point I. Draw in lines AI, IH, and HF to create square AIHF.

If you like, you can then go on to use line IF—the diagonal of the second, larger square—as the side of a new square, which will be four times larger than the first one. This process can be continued indefinitely, or at least until you run out of paper.

Exercise for Emblem 20

For this exercise, you may find graph paper helpful; the ordinary geometer's tools will also be needed. There are many different ways to create a gnomon for any given shape, and each shape has its own rules. In this exercise, we'll concentrate on one way for creating gnomons for squares, partly because the method is a classic one, partly because you can check your work easily with graph paper.

Start by drawing a square of any convenient size; for the sake of the exercise, it's best if this first square has a whole number of graph-paper squares inside it. Then, with the straightedge, draw three additional lines. All three of these start at the same corner of the square—the lower left corner, let's say. The first goes from there through the upper left corner and on as far as the paper allows, extending one side of the square; the second goes from the lower left corner through the lower right one and on to the end of the page, extending another side of the square; the third goes from the lower left corner through the lower right, forming the diagonal of the square, and going on to the edge of the paper as before.

Now take the compass, put the metal point on the lower left corner, and set the width to the distance to the upper right corner, along the diagonal. Swing an arc to either side of the diagonal until it touches the other two lines. Mark points A and B where the arc and the lines intersect. Then, from A and B, draw lines over and up to the diagonal line. These new lines should be parallel to the sides of the original square. (This can be done by geometrical constructions, but for the time being it's simpler to follow the lines of the graph paper.) The two lines should intersect with the diagonal at the same point; mark this as point C. Points A, C, B, and the lower left corner of the original square form a

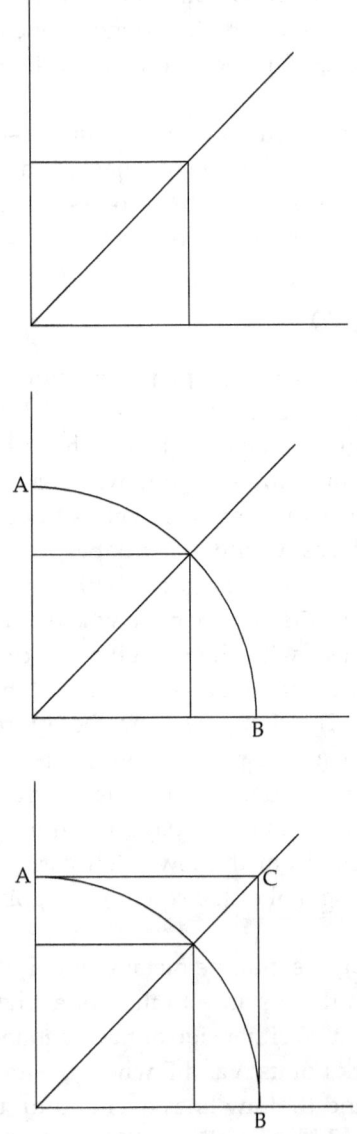

Drawing the gnomonic expansion.

new square larger than the original. (If you've been paying attention, you've probably noticed that the second square uses a version of the square-and-diagonal construction of Emblem 19, and so has twice the area of the first square.)

Do this same construction again, taking the square you just drew in place of the original square. Repeat several times, until you've constructed a series of squares, each one larger than the one before it. The L-shaped areas that expand each square to the next are the gnomons constructed by this method.

Again, there are other ways of making gnomons for squares, some of them of very different shapes. You may find it interesting to try to figure out some of the others, and to work out geometrical ways to create them.

Exercise for Emblem 21

For this exercise, the ordinary geometer's tools and a couple of sheets of blank unlined paper will be used. Start by constructing a square ABCD, using any convenient method; the one introduced in the exercise for Emblem 19 is particularly well suited. Once you have done so, draw a diagonal line from B to C across the square. Then, with the metal point of the compass at point D and the distance between the points set to BD, draw an arc as shown from B to C. Next, place the straightedge on points A and D of the square, and make a mark on line BC, dividing it in half.

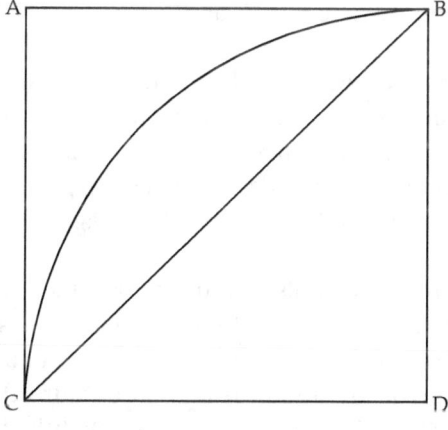

Drawing the spiral.

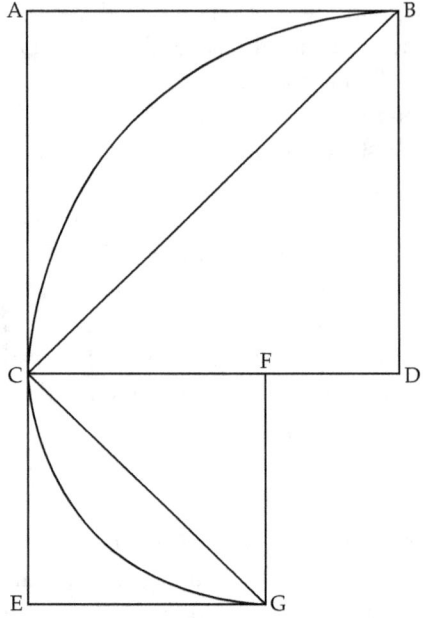

Drawing the spiral.

Then extend line AC down, using the straightedge. Set the compass to half the length of line BC—that is, from either B or C to the mark you made at its center with the straightedge—and with the metal point of the compass on C, mark point E with the pencil point of the compass on the extension of line AC, and point F on line CD. Moving the metal point of the compass to points E and F, make two intersecting marks, locating point G.

Draw in square CFEG. With the straightedge, draw a diagonal line from C to G, and with the metal point of the compass on F, and the width of the compass unchanged, draw an arc from C to G as shown.

You can then repeat the same process again, producing square HJGI, the diagonal line GJ and the arc from GJ, and again as many more times as you wish.

The same process can also be done the other way around, from smaller to larger; in this case, all you have to do is set the compasses each time to the whole length of the diagonal, rather than half its length. This process, as you've doubtless figured out already, creates a spiral defined by the √2 relationship; you can use a slightly different version of the same process, using the width and length of the vesica, to create a √3 spiral, and there are many other similar spirals that can be constructed using variants of the same method.

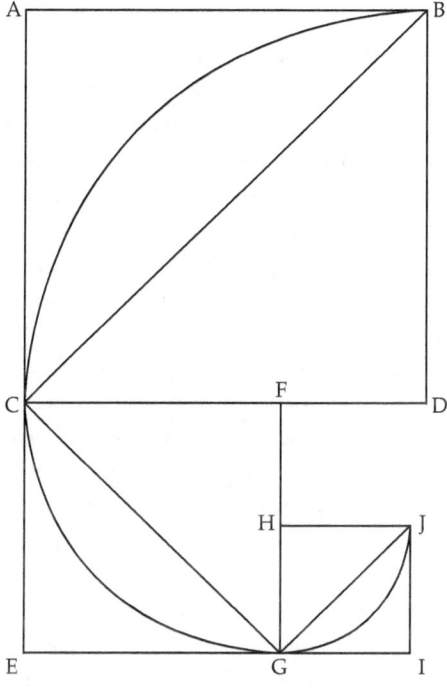

Drawing the spiral.

Exercise for Emblem 22

To put the principle of alternation into practice, we'll make use of an ancient example. Theon of Smyrna was a philosopher, mathematician and sacred geometer who lived in the second century of the Common Era; in his book *Mathematics Useful for Understanding Plato*, he included an example of alternation using the √2 ratio, which we'll follow here. Several pieces of graph paper will be useful.

The goal of this exercise is to create a set of ratios between whole numbers, which will approach closer and closer to the √2 relationship as they proceed. Start by drawing a square on the graph paper, with sides equal to one of the paper's squares. Draw in the diagonal. The side equals 1, and the diagonal falls between 1 and 2; you can check this with another piece of the same graph paper. Since we need whole numbers, we set the diagonal number at 1, a little less than the actual length of the diagonal.

Now Theon's method takes over. Add the side to the diagonal, to get the side of a new square; 1 + 1 = 2, so the second square has sides equal to 2. Now double the side of the original square and add this to the diagonal, to get the diagonal number of the new square; (2 x 1) + 1 = 3, so the new square has a diagonal number of 3. If you draw the second square and measure its diagonal, the actual length is between 2 and 3, so again our figure is less than one unit away from the actual measurement—but this time, it's a little more.

Repeat the same process again. Add the side and the diagonal of the second square, to create the side of a third square: 2 + 3 = 5. Double the side of the second square and add the result to the diagonal, to create the diagonal of the third square: (2 x 2) + 3 = 7. If you draw the new square and measure the diagonal, you'll find that the diagonal of a square with a side equal to 5 has a diagonal between 7 and 8, so—as with the first square—the diagonal measure produced by Theon's method is within 1 of the actual value, but is a little less.

Repeat the same process again, adding the side and the diagonal to get the new side, and doubling the side and adding this to the diagonal to get the new diagonal. 5 + 7 = 12, and (2 x 5) + 7 = 17; the fourth square will have a side of 12 and a diagonal of 17. The actual length of the diagonal falls between 16 and 17, so here again, as with the second square, the diagonal number is a little more than the actual value.

The same operation can be repeated again and again, making ever larger squares, with diagonal numbers that are always within 1 of the actual measure of the diagonal, and alternate between being a little above the correct figure and a little below it. (This is where the term alternation comes from.) If we treat the values of the sides and diagonals as ratios, we get a series of ratios—1:1, 2:3, 5:7, 12:17, 29:41, 70:99, and so on—which come ever closer to the actual ratio between the side and the diagonal of a square, 1:$\sqrt{2}$. These ratios quickly become very close: 99/70, in decimal terms, equals 1.4142857..., while the square root of 2 works out to 1.4142135....

In this way, methods based on alternation allow the sacred geometer to work out number-equivalents for relationships that can't be exactly expressed in number. Patterns similar to Theon's can be used to approximate the $\sqrt{3}$ relationship, as well as the others used in traditional sacred geometry.

Exercise for Emblem 23

This exercise will use blank paper and the ordinary set of geometer's tools. To begin, draw a square, using either the construction from the exercise for Emblem 12 or the one from the exercise for Emblem 19.

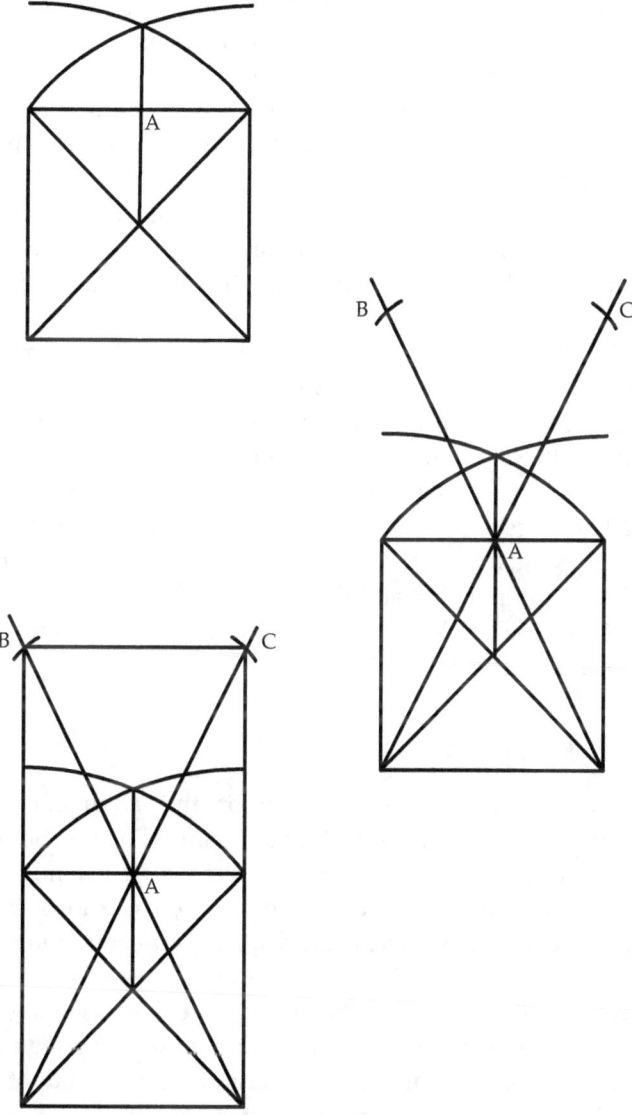

Drawing the double square.

If you use the latter, draw in both of the square's diagonals once the square itself is constructed.

The goal of this exercise is to construct a second square next to the first, and of exactly the same size. Start by putting the metal point of the compass on one of the lower corners of the square, and setting the compass width to the length of the diagonal—that is, to the distance from that corner to the opposite one. Draw an arc up from the opposite corner until it's well past the midpoint of the square's upper side. Then move the metal point of the compass to the other lower corner of the square, and with the compass at the same setting, draw another arc up from the other upper corner, crossing the first arc above the middle of the upper side.

Line up the straightedge on the point where the two arcs cross and the point where the square's two diagonals cross, and draw a line connecting these. Where this line crosses the upper side of the square, mark point A.

Next, leaving the compasses at the same setting, put the metal point on each of the square's upper corners in turn and draw two arcs, of a quarter circle each, in the space above the original square. (It's not necessary for these arcs to cross each other.) Then line up the straightedge on point A and each of the original square's lower corners in turn, drawing two lines, which cross at point A and go out to intersect the two arcs you've just drawn. Where the lines cross the arcs, mark points B and C. Connect points B and C with each other, and with the upper corners of the square below, to form a new square exactly the size of the original one.

Exercise for Emblem 24

In the exercise for this emblem, we'll explore the pattern of progression of roots directly. Start by constructing a square, using the method from the exercise for Emblem 19. Using the straightedge, extend two opposite sides of the square out in the same direction, as shown in the diagram; make sure you extend the lines at least far enough to allow you to draw in another square. For the sake of clarity, we'll label the corners of the square on the side where the lines don't extend as points A and B, and the corners where the lines start their extension as points C and D.

Now put the metal point of the compass on point A, and set the compass width so that the pencil point reaches to point C at the opposite

EXERCISES FOR THE 33 EMBLEMS   149

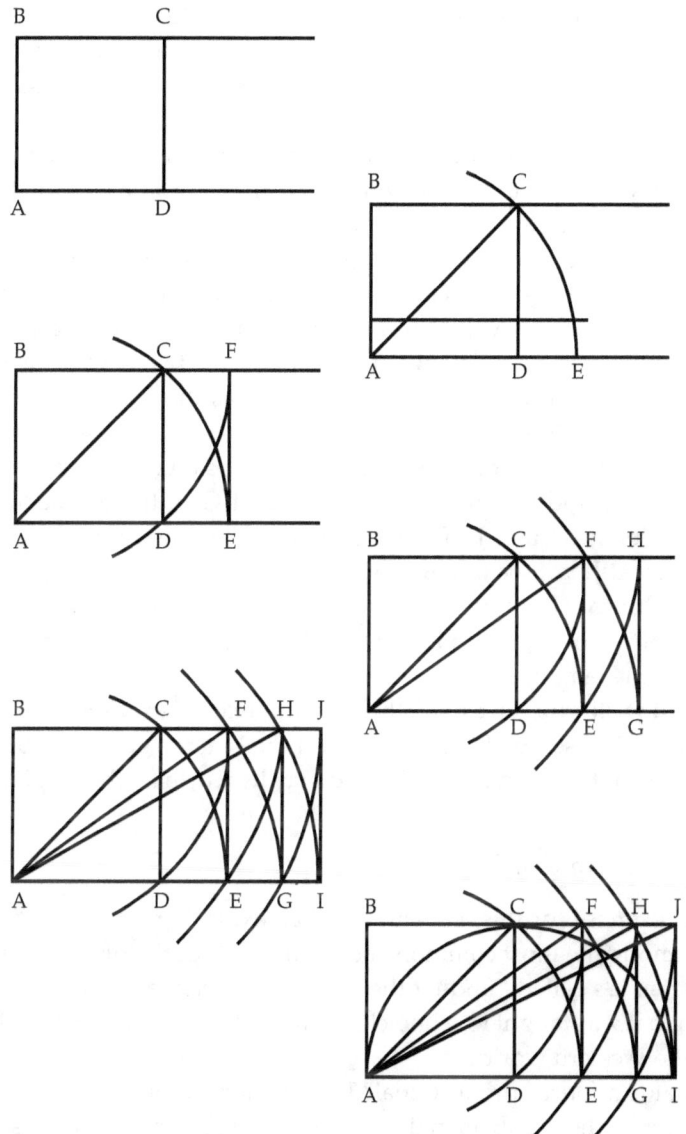

Drawing the progression of roots.

corner of the square, across the diagonal. Draw an arc down from C until it crosses the extended line; mark point E here. Then move the metal point to B, set the pencil point at D, and draw an arc up from D to the extended line. Mark point F where arc and line cross. Draw a line from E to F to complete rectangle ABFE, which is a √2 rectangle—that is, a rectangle where the length relates to the width (or vice versa) in the ratio 1:√2.

Now put the metal point of the compass back on A, set the width to the distance from A to F, and swing an arc down from F to the extended line, marking point G where arc meets line. Move the metal point to B and repeat the process, swinging an arc from E to the line, marking point H. Draw a line from G to H to complete rectangle ABHG, which is a √3 rectangle. (If you want to doublecheck this, construct a vesica piscis with the distance from A to B as the radius of the two circles; the length of the vesica's major axis will be the same as the length of rectangle ABHG's long side.)

Now repeat the process, setting the compass width to the distance from A to H and drawing arcs from H and G to the extended lines, marking points I and J. If you've followed the instructions carefully, rectangle ABJI will be a double square. Check this by setting the compass width to AB, putting the metal point at D, and drawing a semicircle from A through C to I, showing that lines AB, AD, CD, and DI are all the same length.

If you wish, you can extend this further, creating √5, √6, √7, and higher rectangles. These saw little use in traditional sacred geometry, but they have some interesting properties and may be worth further exploration.

Exercise for Emblem 25

As the exercise for this emblem, we'll be exploring a process that was once among the most common and useful tools of the practicing sacred geometer. It's called "finding the fourth proportional," and not all that long ago it was taught to schoolchildren as a basic mathematical skill all over the Western world.

What is a fourth proportional? Imagine for a moment that you only had three of the numbers in the example we used earlier in this section. You have 1 and 2, and you know that the first term of the second pair of numbers is 3…but you don't have the last number. That number is called the fourth proportional.

Working out the fourth proportional in numbers can be done, but it's not always the best approach. If the measurements that you're using happen to be in whole numbers, as in the example just given, you're in

EXERCISES FOR THE 33 EMBLEMS   151

luck; you can solve problems like this easily by using simple mathematics. If the measurements work out to complicated fractions or, worse still, to irrational numbers like √2, you have a lot more work ahead of you. If you use geometry, on the other hand, the process is simple no matter how difficult the numbers may be.

For this exercise you'll want to use graph paper, as it lets you get past the details of construction into the actual process more quickly, and it also allows you to check your work by arithmetic if you want to. (If you've mastered the constructions used in the emblems we've covered up to this point, you can do it on unlined paper; give it a shot if you're feeling confident.) Your geometer's tools are the only other things you'll need.

Start by drawing three lines, all of different lengths, over by one side of the paper. These are your three measurements. Mark them with the letters W, X, and Y. The fourth proportional, the measurement you are trying to find, will be Z.

Now draw another line, at least as long as lines W and Y put together, down the middle of the paper. Use your straightedge, and line it up

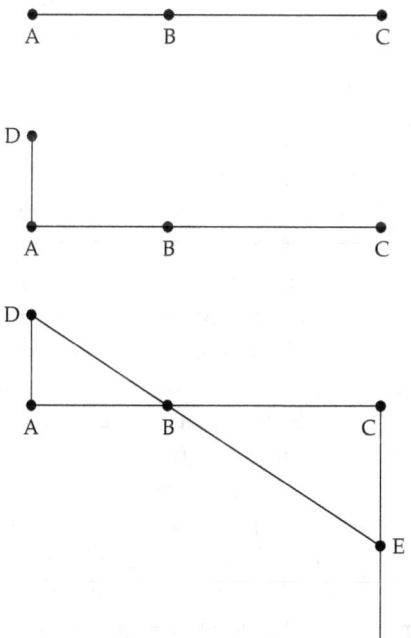

Drawing the discontinuous proportion.

with one of the lines of the graph paper for convenience. Then mark three points, A, B, and C, on the line. A can go anywhere convenient, but should be close to one end of the line. The other two points are placed by measuring: the distance between A and B is the same as the length of line W, and the distance between B and C is the same as the length of line Y. (You can do this by setting the width of the compass points equal to the length of the line, putting the metal point on a point you've already established, and drawing a small arc across the line to show where the other point belongs.)

Then draw a second line, at right angles to the first one, up from point A. (You can construct a right angle geometrically if you wish, or you can simply follow the graph lines.) On this second line, mark point D, so that the distance from A to D is equal to the length of line X. You now have all three of your measurements mapped onto the construction.

At this point, all you have to do is draw another line at right angles to the first line, starting at point C, and going the other direction. Then line up the straightedge on points D and B, and draw a line from D through B to intersect the third line. Mark point E where these two lines intersect. The distance from C to E is the length of the fourth proportional, line Z, which is related to Y in the same ratio as X is to W.

Exercise for Emblem 26

The method of finding the fourth proportional, which was taught in the exercise for Emblem 25, is one of several useful geometrical skills that used to be common knowledge among most people with a basic education. The subject of this exercise is another. It's a method of finding the geometrical mean, and it once saw constant use by artists, architects, designers, and other practitioners of sacred geometry.

What is a geometrical mean? The word mean means "middle," and a mean between two numbers is simply a middle number that relates the two together in some meaningful way. There are various kinds of means. The geometrical mean is another way of talking about the middle term in a continuous proportion where the ratio between the first two terms is the same as that between the last two. In our example above, 1:2::2:4, 2 is the middle term of the proportion, and it can also be described as the geometrical mean between 1 and 4.

This is an easy example, since it involves nothing but whole numbers and a simple proportion. Things can get much more complex when

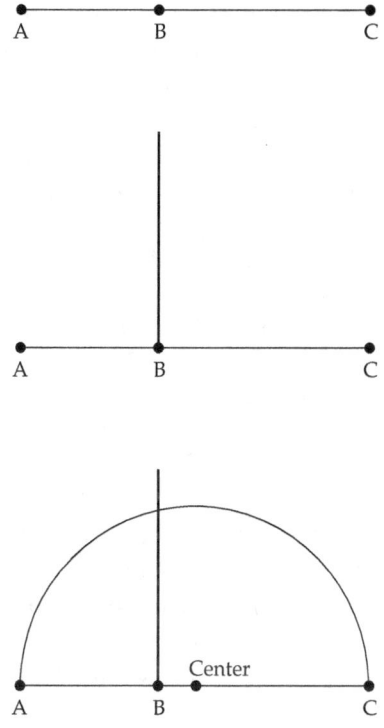

Drawing the continuous proportion.

you're working with relationships like √3 or the Golden Proportion. Trying to deal with these by way of numbers is difficult at best. Again, though, geometry offers an easier way.

For this exercise, as for the last one, graph paper is recommended; the exercise can be done on unlined paper, but graph paper will make it easier for you to check your work. Start by drawing, along one side, two lines of any length you like; for the sake of convenience, one should be a good deal larger than the other, and each one should be an exact number of graph-paper squares in length. (It can be any number of squares you like—14, 9, 33, or whatever—but it shouldn't be 15 and part of a sixteenth, for instance.) Mark the lines as line 1 and line 2.

Now draw a line across the middle of the paper, lining up your straightedge on the grid lines of the graph paper. Mark three points on this line—A, B and C. The distance from point A to point B should be equal to the length of line 1, and the distance from B to C should be the length of line 2. (Use your compass to measure the distance exactly.)

Now, from point B, draw another line at right angles to the original line, and extend it until it's as long as the longer of your two lines.

The next step is to find the center of the whole distance from A to C. You can do this with the construction from the exercise for Emblem 10, or simply "cheat" by counting graph-paper squares. Once you've found and marked the center, put the metal point of the compass there, set the compass width so that the pencil point comes to A, and draw a semicircle around to C, cutting through the other line (the one at right angles to AC) in the process.

Where the semicircle cuts the other line, mark point D. Line BD will be the geometrical mean between line AB and line BC, so that AB, BD, and BC form a continuous proportion.

Exercise for Emblem 27

This exercise will teach another basic construction that was once common knowledge among educated people. The basic Golden Rectangle, with short sides equal to 1 and long sides equal to ϕ, is an essential part of the old traditions of design using sacred geometry. Like the other "irrational numbers" used in the traditional lore, it's surprisingly easy to construct.

Start by drawing a square, using either of the two constructions introduced so far (in the exercises for Emblems 12 and 19). The next step is to divide it in half. One easy way to do this is to construct a vesica, using the two ends of one side of the square as the centers of the circles, and the length of the side as the circles' radius; line up the straightedge on the points of the vesica, and draw the major axis of the vesica, extending it as needed so that it goes through both sides of the square. Mark points A and B where the line intersects the sides of the square.

You now have a square divided into two long rectangles, and if you're paying attention, you've noticed that each of these rectangles is a double square. (Their long sides, after all, are twice the length of their short ones.) Next, put the metal point of the compass on point A and adjust the width until the pencil point is on the opposite corner of one of the rectangles; swing an arc upwards through a quarter circle or so. Move the metal point to B, and swing a second arc up in the same way.

Line the straightedge up on the sides of the original square, and extend the sides up until they intersect the arcs. Where the arcs and lines cross, mark points C and D. Draw in line CD to complete a new rectangle above the square.

This new rectangle is a Golden Rectangle...and so is the rectangle formed by adding the new rectangle to the square! These two rectangles relate to each other, furthermore, by the Golden Proportion; the ratio between the short side of the new rectangle to the side of the square

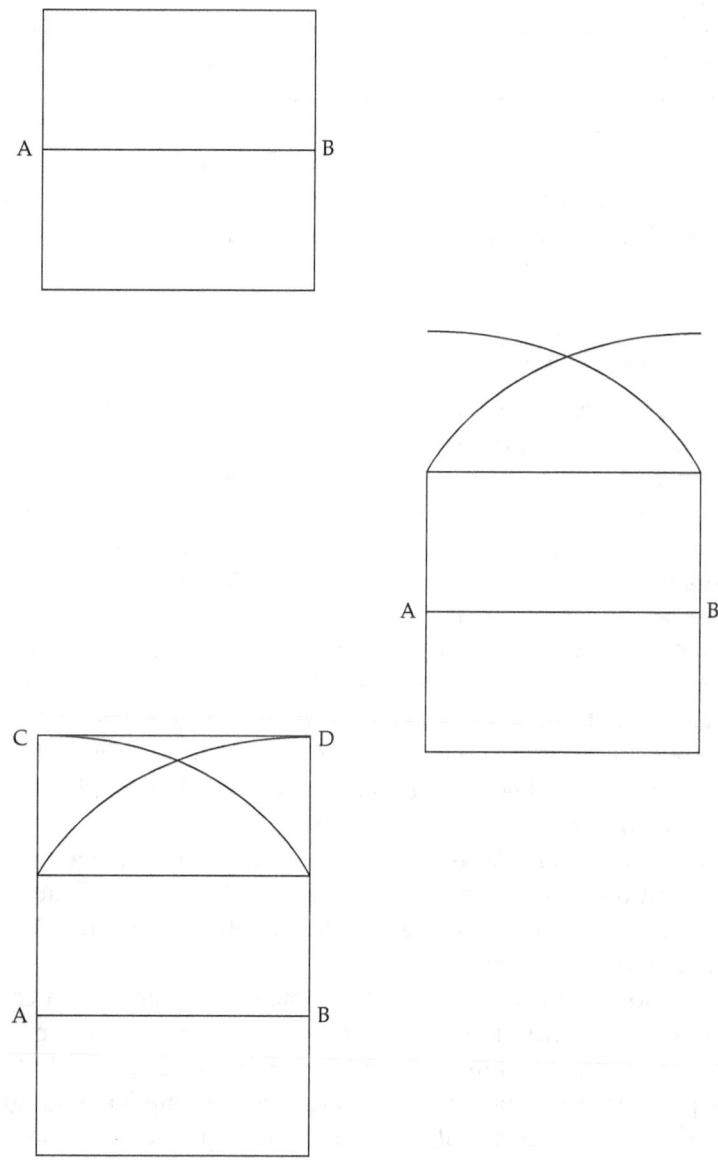

Drawing the Golden Proportion.

is 1:ϕ, and so is the ratio between the side of the square and the side of the combined rectangle, which is made by adding the rectangle's short side to the side of the square—again, a:b::b:(a+b).

If you add another, larger square, with a side equal to the side of the original square plus the short side of the new rectangle, the much larger rectangle formed by the two squares and the rectangle will also be a Golden Rectangle. Similarly, if you take the new rectangle, and cut it into a square as wide as the rectangle's short side and another, leftover rectangle, the leftover rectangle will be another Golden Rectangle. Once you have the basic ratio in place, it's possible to keep on turning out an endless sequence of Golden Rectangles, all of them in perfect proportion to each other, by simply adding or subtracting squares. The Golden Proportion is like that.

Exercise for Emblem 28

For this exercise, the construction of a regular pentagram, start with the method for the quadrature of the circle given in the exercise for Emblem 11. You'll only need to use three of the four points where the cross intersects the circle's circumference—the two ends of the horizontal line, and the upper end of the vertical one. For our present purposes, we'll call the first two points A and B, and the last point C.

Now set the compass to the same setting it was at when you drew the original circle; put the metal point on B, and draw an arc through the center of the circle, swinging it out until it crosses the circumference on both ends, and forming a vesica piscis. At the ends of the vesica's major axis, where the arc and the circle intersect, mark points D and E. Line up the straightedge on these points and draw line DE. Where DE intersects line AB, mark point F.

Put the metal point of the compass on point F and change the compass width until the pencil point comes exactly to point C, up at the top of the circle. From C, draw an arc down until it crosses line AB, and mark point G at the intersection.

Next, move the metal point of the compass to point C, and change the compass width to the distance from C to G. Swing an arc out to either side to the circumference, and mark points H and I. With the metal point on H and the compass setting the same, mark point J further down the circumference; with the metal point on I, do the same thing, marking point K.

EXERCISES FOR THE 33 EMBLEMS 157

Finally, draw in lines CJ, JI, IH, HK, and KC to complete your pentagram.

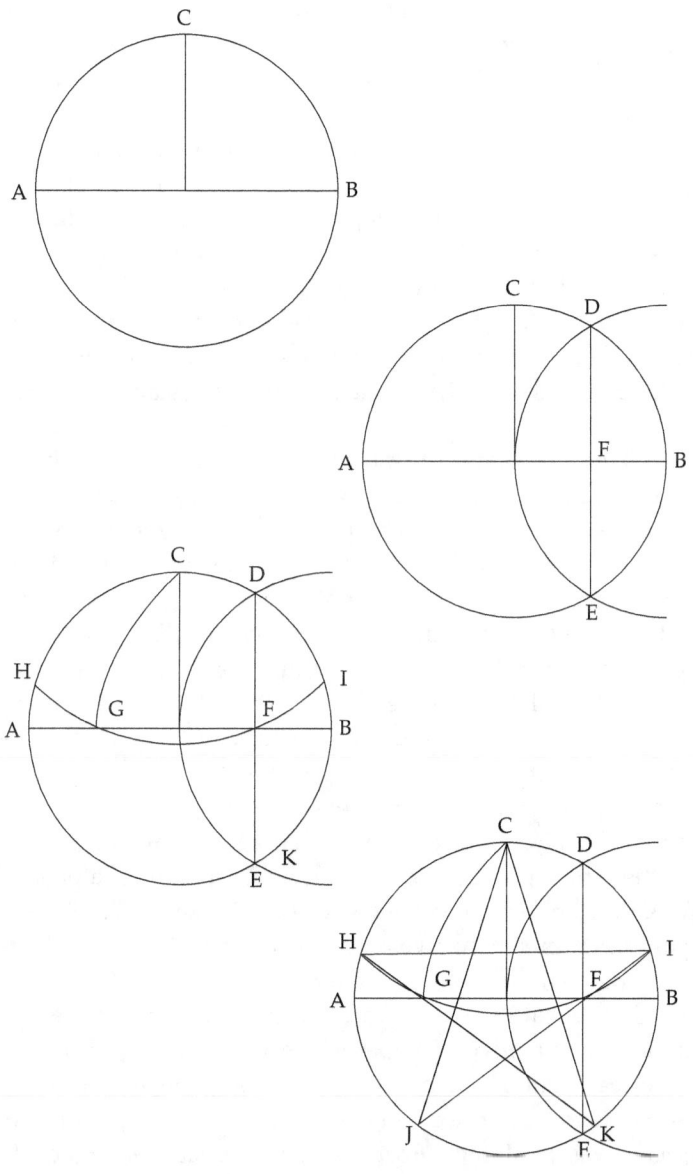

Drawing the pentagram.

Exercise for Emblem 29

This exercise, like those for the other Platonic solids, will require a craft knife or a good pair of scissors as well as the usual geometer's tools, and it's useful to do it on heavier paper than usual; you'll need two sheets this time, as well. This is the most difficult construction you'll be given in this book, but if you follow it step by step you shouldn't have any trouble.

The first step in this construction is to draw a regular pentagon, which you can do by following the instructions for the exercise for Emblem 28, except for the last step of drawing in the pentagram itself. As you start, make sure that the original circle is small enough that you can fit another circle of the same size next to it in any direction without running off the edge of the paper. Instead of the final step, draw in lines CH, HJ, JK, KI, and IC to form the pentagon. You may find it useful to make these lines darker than usual, so that they stand out among the others.

Then set the compass to the radius that you used to make the original circle. Put the metal point on each of the five corners of the pentagon in turn, and draw a circle around each corner. Ignore the part of the circle inside the pentagon. (In fact, you don't even have to draw it.) On the outside, the circles intersect at five points. Mark these as points L, M, N, O and P. Now, without changing the compass setting at all, draw five more circles with the five points you've just marked as the centers. These five new circles will become the framework for five new pentagons.

Next, set the compass to the distance between points C and H—that is, to the length of the side of your original pentagon. Put the metal point of the compass on each of the corners of the pentagon, and draw short arcs to mark in the corners of the new pentagons. (I won't give letters to each of these new points, since we'd quickly run out of alphabet! Simply mark these in the same way you did in the exercise for Emblem 28.) Draw in lines to create the five pentagons around the original one.

When you've done all that, you're halfway there. What you have to do next is to repeat the same process exactly, with the same measurements, on another piece of paper. Once you have two clusters of six pentagons each, cut the clusters out—cut along four sides of each of the outside pentagons, but don't cut them apart from the central one, or you'll have wasted all that effort—bend the outside pentagons up until their edges meet, and tape them together. Finally, join the two halves of the dodecahedron together—the points on each half go into the spaces between the points on the other—and tape. Take the time to study your dodecahedron from various angles, and see the patterns it forms.

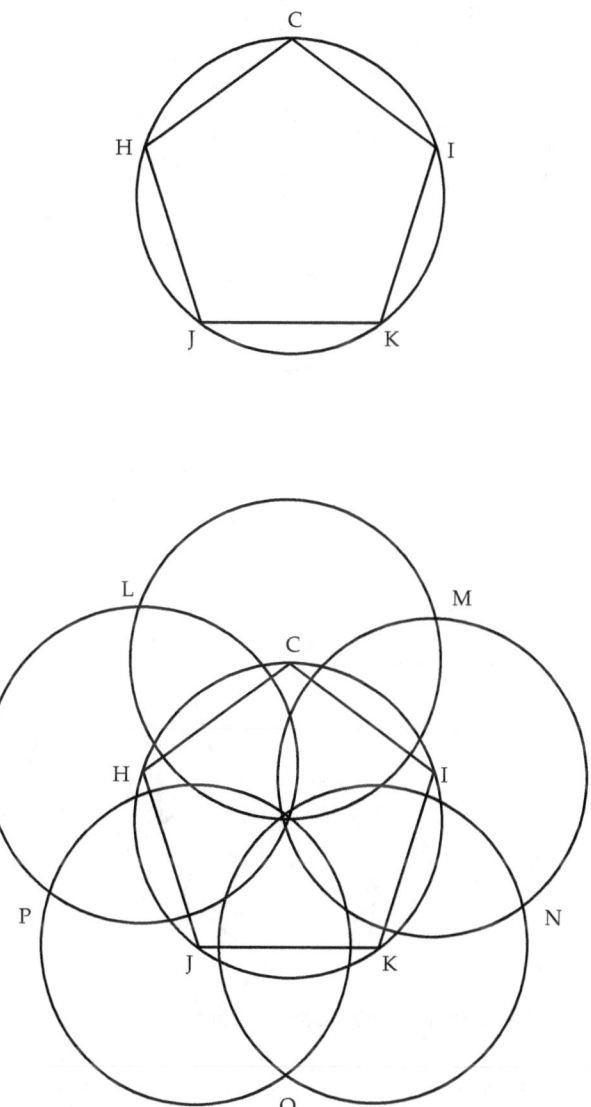

Constructing the dodecahedron.

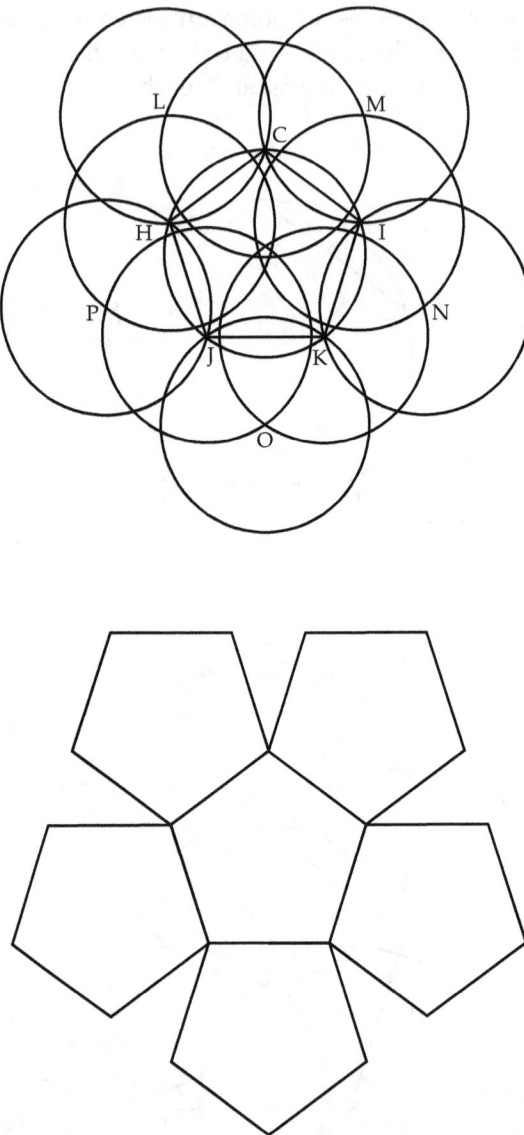

Constructing the dodecahedron. *(Continued)*

Exercise for Emblem 30

The exercise for this emblem involves a simple construction that allows any one of the three fundamental root-relationships to unfold into

EXERCISES FOR THE 33 EMBLEMS   161

the other two. The resulting diagram is an important one, for it sums up many of the principles of traditional sacred geometry in a single

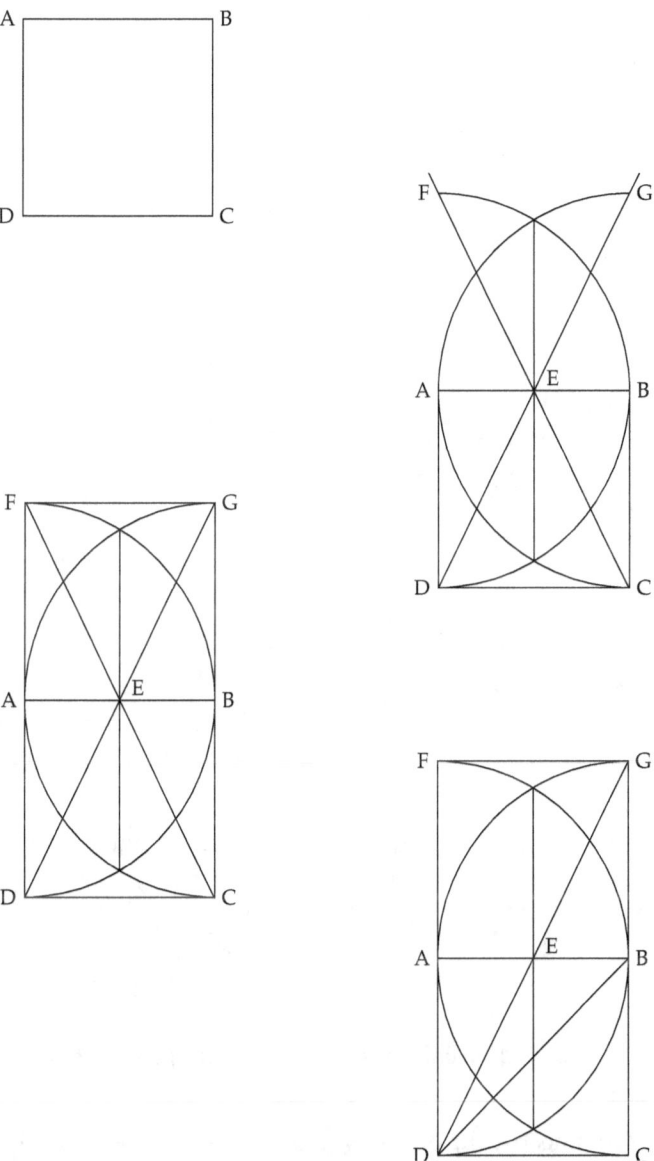

Drawing the unity of the primary roots.

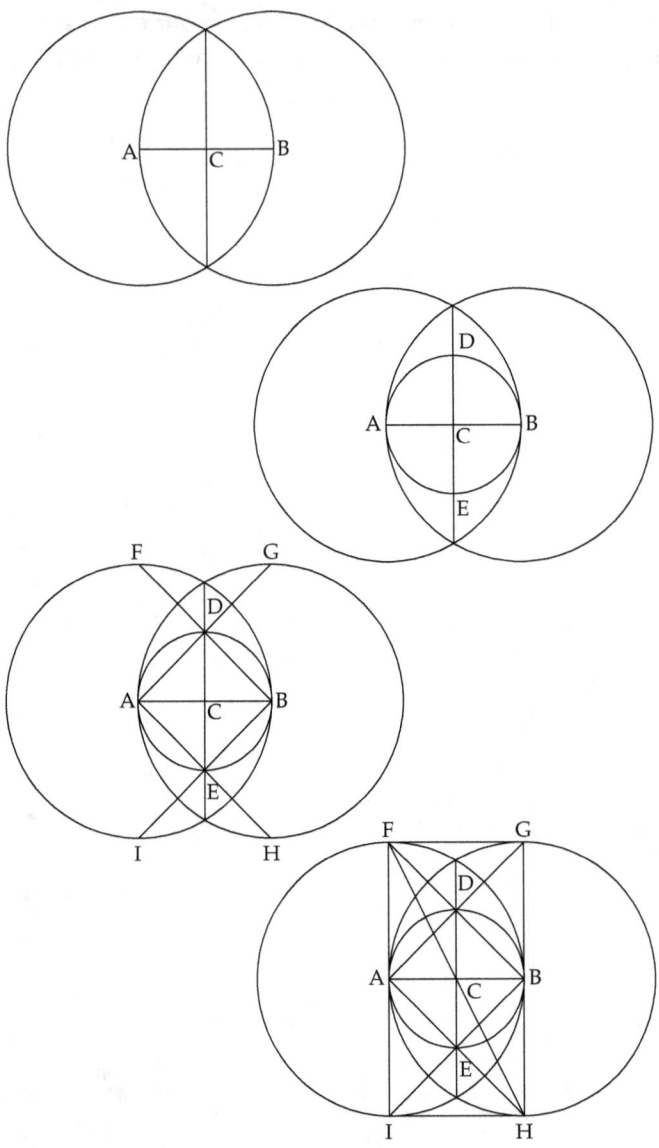

Drawing the unity of the primary roots. *(Continued)*

image. You'll need your ordinary geometer's tools, and several sheets of unlined paper.

There are three ways to start—with a square, with two circles forming a vesica piscis, or with a double square. We'll take these one at a time.

To start from a square, begin by constructing a square, using either of the constructions we've studied so far (the exercises for Emblems 12 and 19 give these). Draw in the diagonal of the square. Choose one side of the square, and label the two corners on that side points A and B; the two on the opposite side are points C and D.

Set the compasses to the distance from A to B, and draw two circles, one with A as center, the other as B, creating the vesica piscis. Draw a line between the two points where the circles cross, dividing line AB in half at point E.

Next, draw a line from point C through point E, and extend it up until it crosses the circumference of one of the circles at point F. Draw another from D through E, and extend it to cross the circumference of the other circle at point G. Draw lines AF, FG, and GB to create the second square ABGF, completing the figure.

To start from a vesica piscis, begin by drawing a vesica according to the construction given in the exercise for Emblem 7. Make the centers of the two circles points A and B. Draw in the major and minor axes of the vesica, and mark point C where they cross. Now put the metal point of the compass on point C, and set the compass width to the distance from C to A. Draw a circle around C, which should pass through both A and B. Where the circle cuts the major axis of the vesica, mark points D and E.

Then draw four lines—from A to D, from A to E, from B to D, and from B to E—extending each of these out to intersect the circumference of one or the other of the two circles. Mark points F, G, H and I where these lines cross the circles. Draw in lines FG, GH, HI, and IF to create both the square and the double square, and draw in line FH to complete the diagram.

To start from a double square, start by constructing a double square as shown in the exercise for Emblem 23. Then simply draw in the diagonal of the lower of the two squares, to give you the $\sqrt{2}$ relationship, and draw in two circles with their centers at the midpoints of the two long sides, and the compass set to the length of the short side, to give you the $\sqrt{3}$. Draw in the major axis of the vesica piscis to complete the diagram.

Exercise for Emblem 31

The Sphere is the one emblem in the Sacred Geometry Oracle for which there's no practical geometrical exercise. The reason for this is simple: there is no way to construct a sphere, or even a really close

164   THE WAY OF THE GOLDEN SECTION

approximation to one, using the tools of the sacred geometer and a sheet of paper. A sphere can have no angles and no flat surfaces; only a pattern with an infinite number of infinitely small sides would do the job—and this is a little hard to carry out in practice!

To explore the sphere, it's necessary to stray out of the boundaries of sacred geometry itself just a little, and venture into another branch of the ancient quadrivium—the fourth branch, astronomy. One good way to do this is to go outside on a clear evening just after sunset, when the moon is in its first quarter and one or more planets will be visible. (You can look this up in any good almanac.) Find a grassy slope with a good view of the western sky, and lay down on your back, looking out into infinite space. Though the sun is below the horizon, you can see its rays streaming upwards from the west, and the crescent of the moon shows that those same rays are illuminating one face of our sister world. If Venus or Mercury are visible, be aware of the sun's rays lighting them also.

As you gaze into the sky, then, try to become aware, not just as an intellectual idea but as an actual experience, that you are on a sphere yourself, spinning through the same heavens as the sun and its other planets. Try to realize, with your whole being, that you are looking out rather than up—that the earth is not a flat surface beneath you but a sphere among spheres, sweeping through space as it turns on its axis—that the sun and moon are not setting, but rather that the part of the earth you're on is turning away from them.

It's a dizzying experience, and you may not want to try to drive immediately afterwards.

Exercise for Emblem 32

There are various traditional methods for squaring the circle to within a few percent of the exact value. The method we'll be using here is among the simpler, and it also has the useful feature of starting on ground we've already covered several times. This particular construction is an ancient one, and has been explored in detail by the modern sacred geometer John Michell.

Begin by marking a point, point A, and drawing a circle of any convenient size around it. Choose a second point, point B, on the circumference of the circle, and draw a circle of the same size around it, creating a vesica piscis. Then draw a line from A to B, extending it out to both

EXERCISES FOR THE 33 EMBLEMS   165

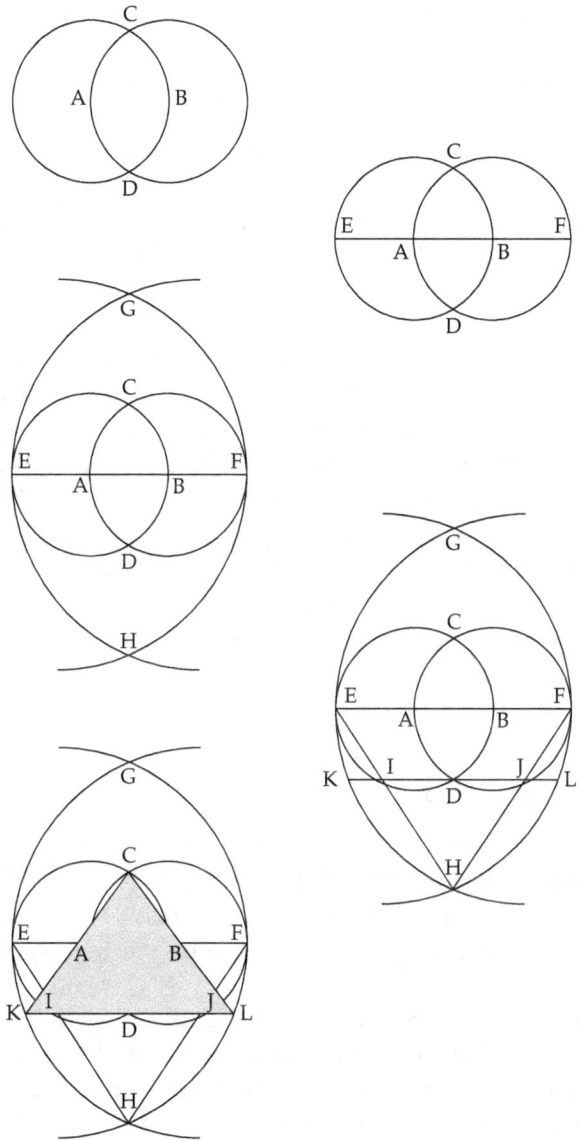

Drawing the squaring of the circle.

sides to touch the circumferences of the circles on either side. Mark points C and D where the circles cross, and points E and F where line AB touches the circumferences.

Next, put the metal point of the compass on E, set the width to the distance from E to F, and draw an arc up and down from point F through at least a third of a circle. Move the metal point to F, and swing an identical arc up and down from E to intersect with the first arc, forming a larger vesica. Mark points G and H where the two arcs cross.

Then draw lines from E and F to H. Where these two lines cross the original circles, mark points I and J. Lining up the straightedge on points I, D, and J, draw a line across the larger vesica out to the arcs on either side. Where this new line touches the arcs, mark points K and L.

If you now construct a square with line KL as its base, using the construction from the exercise for Emblem 20, and draw a circle with C as center and the distance from C to D as radius, you've accomplished one form of squaring the circle—the perimeter of the square will be nearly equal to the circumference of the circle. This diagram has another mystery to reveal, though. If you draw lines from point C to points K and L, the resulting triangle has exactly the same proportions and angles as a vertical section through the Great Pyramid of Giza. Several modern students of sacred geometry have suggested that this, in fact, is one of the secrets hiddin the structure of the enigmatic Egyptian monument.

Exercise for Emblem 33

For this exercise, you'll need the ordinary set of geometer's tools, several sheets of paper, and one other thing—your own body. (You may also find a mirror useful at some points.) There isn't a specific construction involved; rather, your goal is to explore some of the geometries of yourself.

The hand and the face are perhaps the easiest parts of the body to work with, since they are around the same size as the geometrical diagrams with which you've been working. Start by drawing four lines, to represent the fingers, and using the compass to mark off distances equal to the length of the different joints of your fingers. See how the different measures relate to one another. Try making different constructions with one or another measurement as basis—triangles, vesicas, squares with their diagonals, Golden Proportion rectangles, and so on.

Now do the same thing with your face, using a mirror to guide your hand, and being especially careful near the eyes. When your eyes are open to their normal width, how close do they come to perfect vesicas? What are the proportions of your nose, your mouth, your forehead, the line of your jaw? Take these explorations as far as you wish, and be aware that this sort of measurement and calculation was an important part of the training of a sacred geometer in ancient times.

APPENDIX TWO

Meditations on the 33 Emblems

Each of the thirty-three cards of *The Sacred Geometry Oracle* has a meditation associated with it. As with the geometrical exercises, you will need to do each of these meditations at least once before you perform your ritual of self-initiation; they are presented in the book that comes with the Oracle, but are included here also for convenience.

Meditation for Emblem 1: The Unmarked Card

Each of the meditations on the emblems focuses on a particular subject. For Emblem 1, the subject is—nothing at all! Once you've finished the opening process, simply let your mind empty itself of thoughts, and do your best to keep it that way. As soon as you try this, of course, various kinds of mental chatter will spring up to fill the emptiness. Images, ideas, fantasies, worries, things you need to do as soon as the meditation is over and things you should be doing instead of meditating will all come rushing into your mind. This sort of mental static is one of the constants of meditation, at least in the early stages. Contend with it for five minutes or so, and then close as directed in the section on meditation.

Meditation for Emblem 2: The Point

The subject for this meditation is the idea of a geometrical point. Start by imagining a point, all alone in an emptiness that extends in every direction without limit. Let this image build up solidly in your mind's eye, until you can see the point clearly in the middle of infinite space. Now think of the point itself as infinitely small, without length or width or depth—pure position, as the old definition has it, without magnitude. Think about the way these two infinities, the infinitely small in the midst of the infinitely vast, mirror each other. Consider any comments that particularly struck you in the discussion of the emblem above, and see how they relate to the ideas just mentioned. When you've taken them as far as you can, finish in the way described earlier.

Meditation for Emblem 3: The Line

The topic for this meditation is the line. Start by imagining a point in the middle of infinite space, as in the meditation for Emblem 2. When this image is solidly built up in your mind's eye, imagine another point, some distance away from the first one. Try to hold both points at once in your imagination; be aware of the relationship between them, and the endless space opening up to either side.

Then allow a perfectly straight line to form between the points, connecting them and shooting off in both directions past the points toward infinity. Follow the line with your mind's eye in one direction, then the other, then return to the two points and the line connecting them.

Now think about the line and the points it connects, and allow the image to suggest ideas to you. Make use of any ideas that interested you in the discussion of the emblem above. Are there parts of your life that remind you of the interaction between the points and the line? What does that interaction look like from the perspective of each of the points? What about from the perspective of the line? Take this as far as you can, and then close.

Meditation for Emblem 4: The Circle

Here the topic is the circle. Start, as before, by imagining a single point in the midst of infinite space. When this image is built up solidly in your mind's eye, imagine another point some distance away from the first;

hold both of the points in your awareness, being aware of the relationship between them, as you did in the meditation for Emblem 3. This time, however, let the first point be the center, and imagine the second one beginning to move slowly around it in a circle, like a planet orbiting a star. The two points stay exactly the same distance from each other, and the first point does not move at all. Where the second point passes, it leaves a track that you can see, so that as it finishes its first circuit it has traced a circle in space.

As before, begin to think about what this image might mean to you. Think of circles as they appear in folklore and figures of speech, in nature and in human nature. Consider the subject in a general way for a time, then choose one of the possible trains of thought and follow it to its end, returning to the image and then to the train of thought if your mind drifts away from it. Finish the meditation in the usual way.

Meditation for Emblem 5: The Ellipse

After the same opening process as before, imagine a point amid endless space. After the first point is solidly established in your mind's eye, imagine a second point not far away. Then, as in the exercise, imagine an ellipse taking shape around the two points. Try to sense the way the points around the circumference of the ellipse relate to the two foci, by turns closer to one and further from the other.

When this imagery is solidly built up, go on to the next phase, and allow this pattern of images to call up ideas and images in your mind. What does the ellipse seem to symbolize? What meanings might it have? As before, consider these things in a general way for a time, then take one train of thought and follow it out to its end. Finish the meditation in the usual way.

Meditation for Emblem 6: The Vesica Piscis

Begin this meditation with the same opening process as usual. Then start once again by imagining a point in the middle of infinite space. Imagine a second point some distance away from the first, and then, as in the meditation on the circle, picture the second point moving around the first, tracing out a circular track in space. Let the second point circle the first for a time, and then bring it back to its starting place, where it rests. Next, imagine the first point leaving its place and circling the

172   THE WAY OF THE GOLDEN SECTION

second, tracing out a track of its own. This track crosses the one already made by the second point, forming the pattern of the vesica piscis.

Finally, bring the first point back to its starting place, and then imagine both points moving at the same time, each following its own track through space at the same pace. The result is rather like an abstract geometrical dance. As with the meditations you've already done, let these patterns of imagery remind you of things in the universe, your life, and yourself that seem similar to them. Consider these in a general way, and then choose a particular train of thought and follow it as far as you can. Finish the meditation in the usual way.

Meditation for Emblem 7: The Equilateral Triangle

Begin with the same process as before. After you've reached the state of inner clarity, imagine the point in infinite space, and then a second point, some distance away from it. Picture a line going from one to the other. While this line, like all lines, can be extended infinitely out through space, for now pay attention only to the segment uniting the two points.

Next, imagine two more lines of exactly the same length, each one connected to one of the two points but not to the other. Imagine them lying together with the first line, and then pivoting upwards, crossing each other. The third line remains in place, unmoving. The two lines continue to pivot until their ends come into contact. Then they stop, forming a triangle.

As before, allow this pattern of imagery to stir reflections and comparisons in your mind, and draw on any material from the foregoing discussions that seems useful. What does the triangle bring to mind, in the universe, your life, and yourself? Think about it generally for a time, and then choose a train of thought and follow it to the end. Finish in the usual way.

Meditation for Emblem 8: The Hexagram

After the usual process of opening a meditation, imagine a triangle. (If you like, you can create it in the same way as in the last emblem's meditation.) Hold it in your mind's eye for a moment, and then imagine another one exactly equal to it, set so precisely onto the first triangle that it looks as though there's only one triangle there.

Then imagine the second triangle pivoting slowly and gradually, like the hand on a clock face, until it and the first triangle form a hexagram. Hold the image in your mind's eye for a short time. Go on to allow the image to call up images, ideas and associations as before; think about these generally for a time, and then choose a particular train of thought and follow it out to the end. Finish the meditation in the usual way.

Meditation for Emblem 9: The Cross

After the usual opening, imagine a line; if you like, you can start out as before with the point in space and construct the line from it, as in the meditation for Emblem 2. Choose a point on the line, and then imagine another line crossing your first line at right angles.

The cross you've formed consists of two lines, but it also emphasizes one particular point—the point of intersection between the two lines. This has the same symbolic meanings as any point, and brings up an interesting idea. Two points, as we've seen, define a line, but equally, two lines define a point.

This idea is the topic for your meditation. After you've built up the imagery in your mind's eye, recall what you know about points and lines, along with anything useful from the discussion above, and try to grasp what the idea just mentioned implies in the universe, your life, and yourself. Think about it generally for a time, then follow one particular train of thought as far as you can. Finish in the usual way.

Meditation for Emblem 10: The Right Triangle

Start with the usual opening. Go on from there as in the meditation for Emblem 9, by imagining a pair of lines intersecting at right angles, each line stretching out to infinity in both directions. Now, as in the exercise, imagine a pair of points, one on one line, one on the other, and picture in your mind's eye a third line connecting these two. Allow the points to move up and down the lines, one at a time or together, and see the line that connects them forming many different relationships with the two intersecting lines. Each of these relationships makes a right triangle; every one of these triangles is different from the others, but every one has an identical right angle as its base and foundation.

After you've built up this image in your mind's eye and explored it, turn your attention to the ideas of freedom and limitation. How much of a right triangle is free to change? How much of it is not? How does this relate to the universe, your life, and yourself? Use any part of the previous discussion that you find useful.

Meditation for Emblem 11: Quadrature of the Circle

After the usual opening process, imagine a circle; if you like, you can do this following the same process you used in the meditation for Emblem 4. Next, pay attention to the center point of the circle, and then imagine lines extending out of the center point, reaching out to the circle's edge and dividing the circle into four equal parts.

At this point, turn to the topic of the meditation, which is the presence of fourfold patterns in the world we experience. Think of north, south, east and west; spring, summer, fall and winter; dawn, noon, sunset and midnight; birth, life, death, and the after-death state. If you're familiar with the four traditional elements of Western inner spirituality—air, fire, earth, and water—they can be included, and any other fourfold pattern that comes to mind can be added as well. See how these different "quadratures of the circle" echo one another, and seek out the lessons they have to teach about the universe and our place in it.

Meditation for Emblem 12: The Square

After the usual opening, start by visualizing a point in the middle of infinite space, as before. Imagine the point moving a certain distance, leaving a visible track behind it, and forming a line. Next, imagine the line moving sideways, at right angles to the first motion, but covering exactly the same distance. The line leaves a track behind it as well, and this forms a square in space.

When you've built up this image solidly in your mind's eye, move on to the topic, which is the square. Any of the material covered in the discussion above is fair game, but try to think of it in terms of the pattern of images just outlined: the point becoming the line, the line becoming a square. Don't hesitate to draw on your meditations on the point and the line to help you make sense of this pattern.

Meditation for Emblem 13: The Octagram

After the usual opening process, imagine a circle divided into eight even segments. Picture lines reaching out from point to point to form an octagram. Build this imagery up as solidly as possible in your mind's eye. Then go on to think about the topic for this meditation, which is the relation between your freedom and the freedom of others—between the choices you make which affect other people, and the choices made by other people that affect you.

Meditation for Emblem 14: The Dodecagram

After the usual opening process, imagine an equilateral triangle. Once it's solidly built up in your mind's eye, imagine another, pointing in the opposite direction, so that you now have a hexagram. Then imagine a third, pointing off at a right angle to the first two, and finally a fourth, pointing the opposite direction of the third.

Think of the way that the four triangles point in four different directions, and imagine a square that surrounds the four points. Once you've explored the way that the triangles define a square, turn to the topic of this meditation, which is the relation between unity and complexity. The dodecagram is a unity composed of other unities, just like everything else in the universe. What do the individual parts bring to the whole? What does the whole bring to the parts?

Meditation for Emblem 15: The Tetrahedron

After the usual opening process, imagine a tetrahedron—a three-sided pyramid made of equilateral triangles—and build up the image in your mind's eye until the image is solid and stable. (If you've played tabletop roleplaying games, you know this shape as a d4.) At this point, turn to the topic of the meditation, which is the idea of fire. Start with the simple experience of fire—of flame, heat, and light—and go on to think of energy in general and all things "fiery," thinking about how they relate to you and your life. If you're familiar with any of the traditional teachings about the five elements, go ahead and use this material.

Meditation for Emblem 16: The Octahedron

Start with the usual opening. When this is completed, imagine an octahedron. (Gamers will know this as a d8.) Once you've built up the image of the octahedron clearly in your mind's eye, turn to the topic of the meditation, which is the element of air. Think about air, about everything connected with air and everything "airy," drawing on any knowledge of the traditional lore of the elements you happen to have.

Meditation for Emblem 17: The Icosahedron

After the usual opening, imagine an icosahedron. (Gamers will know this as a d20.) When this is clear and solid in your imagination, turn your attention to the topic of the meditation, which is the element of water. Think about water itself, the different kinds of fluid that share water's nature and habits, and all the other things in the universe of your experience that seem "watery" in one way or another. Feel free to relate these to anything you may know about the traditional lore of the elements.

Meditation for Emblem 18: The Cube

After the usual opening process, imagine a cube. (Gamers will know this as a d6.) Then turn to the topic of the meditation, which is the element of earth. Start with the basic, sensory experience of earth—of soil, sand, gravel, rock—and go on from there to think of all things "earthy," exploring how they relate to you and your life. If you've learned any of the traditional teachings about the five elements, make use of these.

Meditation for Emblem 19: Square and Diagonal

After the usual opening, imagine a square; if you wish, you can use the same process as in the meditation for Emblem 12, extending a point into a line and the line into a square. Once the square is built up solidly in your mind's eye, imagine the diagonal being drawn in. From this, unfold the second, larger square, as in the exercise above. When you have built this up solidly in your mind's eye, turn to the topic for the meditation, which is creation by division. Explore this idea in the light of any ideas that seem useful.

Meditation for Emblem 20: Gnomonic Expansion

After the usual opening process, imagine a small square. Add an L-shaped piece to it so that it becomes a larger square. Repeat the process again and again, creating ever larger squares. When this pattern of imagery is built up solidly in your mind's eye, turn your attention to the topic of the meditation, which is the relation between the large and the small. Draw on examples from your own knowledge and experience.

Meditation for Emblem 21: The Spiral

After the opening, imagine a point in the middle of endless space. See it turning around itself, slowly, in the midst of immensity. Then imagine an arc spiralling out from it, growing wider with each turn, reaching out to a great distance. Finally, imagine the same arc turning and spiralling back inwards, cutting across the first spiral as it spins back to the center.

When this pattern of imagery is built up solidly in your mind's eye, turn your attention to the next phase of this meditation, and allow images and ideas suggested by the spiral to take shape in your mind. Be sure to think about both the expanding and the contracting spirals, for each has its lessons.

Meditation for Emblem 22: Alternation

After the usual opening process, imagine a circle. Then imagine two circles side by side inside the first circle; then two more inside each of the smaller circles; then two more side by side inside these. Continue until the circles have become so small that they form what looks like a straight line across the center of the original circle.

When this pattern of images is built up solidly in your mind's eye, go on to the topic of the meditation, which is the relation between perfection and imperfection in the reality we experience around us. Use the idea of alternation to explore this. As before, consider the topic in a general way for a time, then take one train of thought and follow it out to its end. Finish the meditation in the usual way.

Meditation for Emblem 23: The Double Square

After the usual opening, imagine a square. Once this is built up solidly in your mind's eye, imagine a second square above the first, as in the emblem, and the single diagonal that connects them. Consider this image for a time, and then turn to the topic of this meditation, which is the concept of regeneration—the possibility of a transformation that passes beyond the current limits of the self.

178   THE WAY OF THE GOLDEN SECTION

Meditation for Emblem 24: Progression of Roots

After the usual opening process, imagine a square. Exactly as in the exercise for this emblem, which is given on page 149, imagine the square unfolding into a √2 rectangle, a √3 rectangle, and a double square with its diagonal. Then turn your attention to the topic of this meditation, which is the way these three factors proceed from one another. The √2 rectangle stands for generation, the √3 rectangle for relation, and the double square with its √5 diagonal for regeneration; think about these three words and their meanings, and relate them and their geometrical figures together.

Meditation for Emblem 25: Discontinuous Proportion

After the usual opening process, imagine any simple geometric figure you wish. Build it up solidly in your mind's eye. Then imagine it becoming first larger, then smaller, in such a way that it keeps exactly the same shape, and every part stays in the same relationship to every other part. Once you have imagined this clearly, turn to the topic of the meditation, which is the relation between change and stability. See what the image has to say to the experiences you've had in life of things that change, and of things that don't seem to change.

Meditation for Emblem 26: Continuous Proportion

After the usual opening, imagine a simple geometrical shape—a square, a triangle, a circle, or what have you. Build it up solidly in your mind's eye. Then imagine yourself moving closer to it, and discovering that it is made up of smaller versions of the same shape, clustering together. You come closer and closer, and the smaller shapes prove to be made of even smaller ones, themselves made of still smaller ones, and so on as far as your imagination will reach.

Turn to the topic of the meditation, which is the concept of interrelation. A common theme of spiritual teachings from around the world is that all things are interconnected. Think about this, and in particular about situations in your own life where interconnections show themselves.

Meditation for Emblem 27: The Golden Proportion

After the usual opening process, imagine the Golden Rectangle shown on the emblem; leave out the lines and arc inside the rectangle, and just try to pay attention to the overall shape. Consider it, turning it over in your mind and trying to feel how the sides relate to one another. When this is clearly built up in your imagination, turn to the topic of the meditation, which is the idea of beauty. What is beauty? What do we mean when we say that something is beautiful? Is beauty just a matter of perception by the sense, or is there something else involved?

Meditation for Emblem 28: The Pentagram

After the usual opening process, imagine a circle. Then, tracing one line at a time, imagine a pentagram taking shape inside the circle. When this image has been built up solidly in your mind's eye, go on to the topic of the meditation, which is the idea of power. Explore what power means to you, what you would do if you had it. Then consider asking yourself why it is that you think that you don't have it.

Meditation for Emblem 29: The Dodecahedron

Start with the usual opening process, and then imagine a dodecahedron. (Gamers will know this as a d12.) Be aware that you can only see one side of it, and another side, the exact mirror image of the first, is hidden behind the side you can see. Once this imagery is solidly established, go on to the topic of the meditation, which is the idea of spirit. Think of what this means to you, how it relates to the world of your experience, and how it relates to the patterns of the four elements—the patterns you explored in your meditations on Emblems 15, 16, 17 and 18.

Meditation for Emblem 30: Unity of the Primary Roots

After the usual opening process, build up, in your mind's eye, the diagram shown on the emblem. Try to imagine it as clearly and exactly as possible, and see how the square, the vesica, and the double square interact. When you've established this pattern of imagery firmly in your imagination, turn you attention to the topic of the meditation, which is the links among the three root-relationships—$\sqrt{2}$, $\sqrt{3}$, and $\sqrt{5}$—and the three corresponding principles of generation, relation, and regeneration. This is like the meditation for Emblem 24, but you're not limited to the sequence in which these three roots unfold in that diagram.

Meditation for Emblem 31: The Sphere

After the usual opening process, imagine a sphere taking shape around you, extending perhaps a yard or so out from you. Try to build up the image of the sphere surrounding you as solidly as possible in your mind's eye. When you've done this, imagine the sphere getting slowly bigger, expanding to surround the room, your home, your neighborhood, your state or province, your country, your continent, your planet. Allow it to keep getting steadily bigger, until it contains the whole universe. Then release the image. At this point, turn your attention to the topic of this meditation, which is the idea of the universe itself. The word "universe" comes from the Latin *universus*, "that which turns as one." Think about this, and about the things you know or believe about the universe that surrounds you.

Meditation for Emblem 32: Squaring the Circle

After the usual opening process, imagine a circle in the midst of endless space. Once this is built up solidly in your mind's eye, imagine a square below it. The square and the circle are the same relative sizes as the ones in the emblem. After a time, imagine the square rising and the circle lowering, until they overlap exactly. Then turn your attention to the topic of the meditation, which is the relation between spirit and matter. Just as many different forms and functions in sacred geometry are used in different methods of squaring the circle, so a great deal of the material we've covered elsewhere in this book has relevance here.

Meditation for Emblem 33: The Human Canon

After the usual opening process, imagine a circle and a square, as in the last exercise, but already overlapping as in the artwork on Emblem 33. When this image has been built up solidly in your mind's eye, imagine yourself in the center of the diagram. You should picture yourself naked, and try to make the image as exact as possible. If you don't have a very good idea of what you look like with your clothes off, a few minutes of privacy before the meditation in a room with a full-length mirror should solve the problem.

When this whole pattern of imagery is firmly established, turn your attention to the topic of the meditation, which is—yourself! Think about who and what you are; try to get past simple verbal labels—"I am a woman," "I am a man," "I am thin," "I am fat," "I am (fill in the blank)"—toward something deeper and less arbitrary, founded not on words but on experience. Who are you? What are you? Let the questions turn over in your mind, and seek a sense of your own nature. Go on as long as it seems productive, then finish the meditation in the usual way.

RESOURCES

Occultism resources

These books will be especially useful to initiates of the Golden Section Fellowship who want to know more about occultism and the deeper dimensions of the Fellowship's work:

Fortune, Dion, *Aspects of Occultism* (York Beach, ME: Weiser, 2000).
———, *Sane Occultism* (Wellingborough, UK: Aquarian, 1987).
Greer, John Michael, *Mystery Teachings from the Living Earth* (San Francisco, CA: Red Wheel/Weiser, 2012).
———, *The Secret of the Temple* (Woodbury, MN: Llewellyn, 2016).
Hall, Manly Palmer, *Man: The Grand Symbol of the Mysteries* (Los Angeles, CA: Philosophical Research Society, 1982).
———, *Self-Unfoldment by Disciplines of Realization* (Los Angeles, CA: Philosophical Research Society, 1942).
Michell, John, *The New View Over Atlantis* (Newburyport, MA: Hampton Roads, 2013).
Pennick, Nigel, *The Ancient Science of Geomancy* (London: Thames and Hudson, 1979).
Sadhu, Mouni, *Concentration* (North Hollywood, CA: Wilshire, 1959).

Steiner, Rudolf, *How To Know Higher Worlds* (Hudson, NY: Anthroposophic Press, 1994).
Weston, Jessie, *From Ritual to Romance* (Gloucester, MA: Peter French, 1983).

Sacred geometry resources

These are among the books I've found most useful for learning sacred geometry and getting a sense of its deeper aspects and underlying philosophy:

Critchlow, Keith, *Order in Space* (London: Thames & Hudson, 1969).
———, *Time Stands Still* (London: Gordon Fraser, 1979).
Doczi, Györgi, *The Power of Limits: Proportional Harmonies in Nature, Art, and Architecture* (Boston, MA: Shambhala, 1981).
Ghyka, Matila, *The Geometry of Art and Life* (New York: Dover, 1977).
———, *The Golden Number* (Rochester, VT: Inner Traditions, 2016).
Hambidge, Jay, *The Elements of Dynamic Symmetry* (New York: Dover, 1967).
Hersey, George, *Architecture and Geometry in the Age of the Baroque* (Chicago: University of Chicago Press, 2000).
Huntley, H.E., *The Divine Proportion: A Study in Mathematical Beauty* (New York: Dover Books, 1970).
Lawlor, Robert, *Sacred Geometry: Principles and Practice* (London: Thames & Hudson, 1982).
Lundy, Miranda, *Sacred Geometry* (Presteigne, Wales: Wooden Books, 2002).
Michell, John, *City of Revelation* (New York: Ballantine, 1977).
———, *How the World Is Made: The Story of Creation according to Sacred Geometry* (Rochester, VT: Inner Traditions, 2009).
———, *The Dimensions of Paradise: The Proportions and Symbolic Numbers of Ancient Cosmology* (San Francisco: Harper & Row, 1988).
Olsen, Scott, *The Golden Section: Nature's Greatest Secret* (Presteigne, Wales: Wooden Books, 2009).
Padovan, Richard, *Proportion: Science, Philosophy, Architecture* (London: Spon Press, 1999).
Schwaller de Lubicz, R. A., *The Temple of Man* (Rochester, VT: Inner Traditions, 1999).
Stirling, William, *The Canon* (repr. York Beach, ME: Samuel Weiser, 1999).
Sutton, Andrew, *Ruler and Compass: Practical Geometric Construction* (Presteigne, Wales: Wooden Books, 2009).
Sutton, Daud, *Platonic and Archimedean Solids* (Presteigne, Wales: Wooden Books, 2001).

Vandenbrouck, André, *Philosophical Geometry* (Rochester, VT: Inner Traditions, 1987).
Vitruvius Pollio, Marcus, *The Ten Books on Architecture* (New York: Dover, 1960).

Body practice resources

Some body practices can be learned from books and websites, others need to be learned from properly trained teachers. I've offered some hints below, as well as some sources for study.

Aikido

There are several different styles and lineages of aikido, and no one site online gives access to all of them. You can consult an online map program to find dojos (training halls) near where you live. The following books will give you some sense of the art:

Stevens, John, *Aikido: the Way of Harmony* (Boston, MA: Shambhala, 1984).
Westbrook, Adele, and Oscar Ratti, *Aikido and the Dynamic Sphere* (Rutland, VT: Tuttle, 1970).

Do-In

As of this writing the best books on Do-In are out of print, but can very often be found for reasonable prices on the used book market. Some good examples are:

de Langre, Jacques, *The First Book of Do-In* (Magalia, CA: Happiness Press, 1971).
———, *The Second Book of Do-In (Do-In 2)*, (Magalia, CA: Happiness Press, 1974).
Rofidal, Jean, *Do.In: Eastern Massage and Yoga Techniques* (Wellingborough, UK: Thorsons, 1981).

Five Tibetan rites

Peter Kelder's original book, *The Eye of Revelation*, is readily available online and in several reprinted editions, and occult texts such as Donald

Michael Kraig's *Modern Magick* also give detailed instructions in it. The first publication was:

Kelder, Peter, *The Eye of Revelation* (Los Angeles, CA: The Mid-Day Press, 1939).

Hatha yoga

There are literally hundreds of different styles of hatha yoga currently being taught in the Western world, and tens of thousands of books on the subject, hundreds of them well suited to beginners. You should be able to find classes for beginners in your community, either through a yoga school or through some other community organization. If you prefer to learn from books, the the first one listed below is very well suited to older (and less flexible) adults, and the two that follow are widely considered classics:

Christensen, Alice, *Easy Does It Yoga* (New York: Simon & Schuster, 1999).
Iyengar, B.K.S., *Yoga:The Path to Holistic Health* (New York: DK Publications, 2014).
Satchidananda, Sri Swami, *Integral Yoga Hatha* (Buckingham, VA: Integral Yoga Publications, 1970).

Shintaido

You can find the nearest Shintaido dojo to you, and learn something about the art, online at www.shintaido.org. Books worth reading to get a sense of Shintaido include:

Aoki, Hiroyuki, *Shintaido: A New Art of Movement and Life Expression* (San Francisco, CA: Shintaido of America, 1982).
———, *Total Stick Fighting: Shintaido Bojutsu* (Tokyo: Kodansha, 2000).

Tai Chi Chih

The website at www.taichichih.org includes information about this body practice and a roster of accredited teachers. The standard textbook is still the one written by the originator:

Stone, Justin F., *T'ai Chi Chih! Joy Thru Movement* (Santa Barbara, CA: Satori Resources, 1984).

INDEX

affirmations, 31–33, 108
aikido, 84
altar, 36–39, 88, 104–107
Ancient Order of Druids in America (AODA), xi–xii
Ashley, Juliet, xi–xiii, 41–42, 45
astral plane, 75–76
astrology, 108
Awyr, 10, 18

Byw, 14–15, 18

Calas, 7, 9, 18, 21, 80
Carroll, Lewis, 94
Composition of Place, 104

Daear, 12, 18
devil worship, ix
discursive meditation, xiv, 21, 25–26, 28, 35, 63–75, 98, 169–181
divination, 29–30, 98
Do-In, 72, 84

Dolmen Arch, The, 3
Druid Magic Handbook, The, 3, 112
Druidry, xi, 91
Dŵr, 11, 18

egregor, x
Egypt, ix, 66
evening exercise, 27–28, 98, 108

Five Tibetan Rites, 84–85
Fortune, Dion, 70
Fourfold Breath, 68–69

Gates, Seven, 9–15, 42, 94
Gilbert, John, xii, 41–42
Gospel according to John, 70
Gwyar, 8–9, 18, 22, 80

Hall, Manly P., xi
hatha yoga, 85
Holy Grail, 20
Holy Order of the Golden Dawn, xii

illumination, phase of, 22
initiation, 22–23, 35, 97–114
interiorization, phase of, 21–22

journaling, 33–34, 108

kundalini, 113

Lawlor, Robert, xiii
Lévi, Eliphas, 70
life force, 6–7
lodge, 36–39, 87–95, 98, 103–107, 113–114
lunar current, 19–20

Maen, 13, 18
magic, 2–3
Manchester, James, xi
Michell, John, xii
morning exercise, 26–27, 98, 108–109
Murray, Colin, xiii

Nef, 14, 18
New Celtic Review, xiii
Nwyfre, 8–9, 18, 22, 80

objective mind, 3, 20–21, 112
Occult Philosophy Workbook, The, 70
One Life, the, 6–7, 18, 65, 113
Order of Modern Essenes, xii
Order of Spiritual Alchemy, xii
Outer Emblem of the Fellowship, 17–18, 99–104

pineal gland, 113
prayer, 29, 42–43, 71–72

preparation, phase of, 21–22
Principles, Three, 7–9, 88, 92, 94

religion, ix–x, 2, 42

sacred geometry, xii–xiii, 38, 65, 80, 92, 97, 99, 102, 108, 116
Sacred Geometry Oracle, xiv, 15–17, 26, 29, 35, 79, 80–81, 98–99, 103, 107, 115–181
Schwaller de Lubicz, R.A., xii
scrying, 75–81, 98
self-massage, 72–73
Shaw, Matthew, xii–xiii
shintaido, 85
solar current, 19
solar plexus, 3, 21, 28–29, 112
solar plexus exercise, 28–29, 91, 108
Sphere of Protection, xiv, 25–26, 41–62, 65, 91, 98, 109–113
subjective mind, 3–4, 20–21, 112
Symanski, Owen, xii
symbols, 2, 4–5, 98

Tai Chi Chih, 85
Tao Te Ching, 70
tarot, 30, 70–71
telluric current, 19
Theosophical Society, xi
Three Rays of Light, 91

Ufel, 11–12, 18
Universal Gnostic Church, xii, 41–42

vagus nerve, 113

Zasluchy, Omar, xii

www.ingramcontent.com/pod-product-compliance
Lightning Source LLC
Chambersburg PA
CBHW070357240426
43671CB00013BA/2539